Cambridge Elements

Elements in Evolutionary Economics
edited by
John Foster
University of Queensland
Jason Potts
RMIT University
Isabel Almudi
University of Zaragoza
Francisco Fatas-Villafranca
University of Zaragoza
David A. Harper
New York University

EVOLUTIONARY PRICE THEORY

Harry Bloch
Curtin University

CAMBRIDGE UNIVERSITY PRESS

Shaftesbury Road, Cambridge CB2 8EA, United Kingdom

One Liberty Plaza, 20th Floor, New York, NY 10006, USA

477 Williamstown Road, Port Melbourne, VIC 3207, Australia

314–321, 3rd Floor, Plot 3, Splendor Forum, Jasola District Centre,
New Delhi – 110025, India

103 Penang Road, #05–06/07, Visioncrest Commercial, Singapore 238467

Cambridge University Press is part of Cambridge University Press & Assessment,
a department of the University of Cambridge.

We share the University's mission to contribute to society through the pursuit of
education, learning and research at the highest international levels of excellence.

www.cambridge.org
Information on this title: www.cambridge.org/9781009669221

DOI: 10.1017/9781009669184

© Harry Bloch 2025

This publication is in copyright. Subject to statutory exception and to the provisions
of relevant collective licensing agreements, no reproduction of any part may take
place without the written permission of Cambridge University Press & Assessment.

When citing this work, please include a reference to the DOI 10.1017/9781009669184

First published 2025

A catalogue record for this publication is available from the British Library

ISBN 978-1-009-66922-1 Hardback
ISBN 978-1-009-66920-7 Paperback
ISSN 2514-3573 (online)
ISSN 2514-3581 (print)

Cambridge University Press & Assessment has no responsibility for the persistence
or accuracy of URLs for external or third-party internet websites referred to in this
publication and does not guarantee that any content on such websites is, or will
remain, accurate or appropriate.

For EU product safety concerns, contact us at Calle de José Abascal, 56, 1°, 28003
Madrid, Spain, or email eugpsr@cambridge.org

Evolutionary Price Theory

Elements in Evolutionary Economics

DOI: 10.1017/9781009669184
First published online: May 2025

Harry Bloch
Curtin University
Author for correspondence: Harry Bloch, h.bloch@curtin.edu.au

Abstract: Economic evolution involves structural change from within, so evolutionary price theory needs to address how prices facilitate and accommodate this structural change and how structural change in turn impacts prices. Such analysis is impossible using neoclassical price theory in which endowments of inputs, production technology, and consumer preferences are all treated as exogenously determined and the future is known or at least its probability distribution is known. An alternative theory of price determination outlined in this Element is compatible with structural change from within and an unknown future. The theory employs an open-system ontology and a micro-meso-macro methodology. Prices have a dual informational role in evolutionary economics. As well as coordinating ongoing production and consumption activities, prices provide information to guide potential entrepreneurs and their financiers in evaluating the profitability of innovations. The latter role can substantially disrupt the order created in the former role.

Keywords: price theory, evolutionary economics, Schumpeter, creative destruction, structural change

© Harry Bloch 2025

ISBNs: 9781009669221 (HB), 9781009669207 (PB), 9781009669184 (OC)
ISSNs: 2514-3573 (online), 2514-3581 (print)

Contents

Preface	1
1 Introduction	2
Part I Micro	5
2 Consumers	5
3 Firms	11
Part II Meso	28
4 Market Order	28
5 Disrupted Markets and Differential Firm Growth	38
Part III Macro	55
6 Price Linkages and Structural Change	55
7 Waves of Innovation and Price Movements	70
8 Summary and Topics for Further Research	81
References	89

Preface

This Element is the culmination of a long journey of discovery. Ideas from an array of authors across many schools of economic thought are referenced. Novelty is in the way the ideas are synthesised for developing evolutionary price theory. As is appropriate for an evolutionary approach to economics, the whole is greater than the sum of the parts.

I was introduced to anti-trust economics as an undergraduate student by Geoff Shepherd at the University of Michigan. George Stigler strongly prosecuted an opposing view when I was a graduate student at the University of Chicago. Both Shepherd and Stigler mentioned Schumpeter, but neither seriously addressed Schumpeter's critique of equilibrium economics as being tangential to understanding the process of development under capitalism.

My focus as an early career academic was on empirical research into aspects of competition, including pricing, productivity, profitability, industry structure, and advertising. Increasingly, this research identified phenomena not easily explained by mainstream analysis, such as variance in firm size, large productivity differences among firms producing similar products, rigidity in manufacturing prices in response to fluctuating demand, and a long-term downward trend in the ratio of the prices of primary products to those of manufacturing goods. Initially, I turned to post-Keynesian price theory for explanations, but this theory has a short-run orientation that generally doesn't address structural change.

My colleagues at the University of Denver in the early 1980s, especially David Levine, introduced me to Josef Steindl's (Steindl [1952] 1976) analysis of maturity and stagnation in modern capitalism. There are interesting parallels and contrasts between Steindl and Schumpeter in the analysis of competition as a process of differential firm growth following innovations, which I started to explore. However, it wasn't until 1998 that I presented a paper based on comparing the analysis of competition in Schumpeter and Steindl at the International Schumpeter Society conference in Vienna.

Schumpeter Society conferences provided an ideal forum for developing my ideas about evolutionary price theory. My own presentations generated much constructive feedback, while the presentations of others broadened my understanding of evolutionary analysis. Contacts made at the conferences expanded my network for exchanging ideas and draft papers.

Development of my ideas on evolutionary price theory also benefitted from feedback at presentations to groups beyond evolutionary economics. Presentations to the History of Economic Thought Society of Australia and the Society of Heterodox Economists elicited comments encouraging both clarifications and extensions to incorporate diverse insights. I also benefitted from comments at seminars given at an array of universities and research institutes across the globe.

I owe a special debt of gratitude to co-authors on research containing the nascent ideas forming my approach to evolutionary price theory. Thanks go to Jerry Courvisanos, John Finch, Peter Kriesler, Stan Metcalfe, and David Sapsford. Stan has also commented on drafts of several chapters as well as providing advice and encouragement on the whole project. Curtis Eaton, Peter Earl, and John Foster have read chapters and provided very useful feedback, while Margaret Bloch has cast the editor's eye over many of the chapters. None of my dear friends who have helped with the development and exposition of my ideas on evolutionary price theory throughout the many years of its development are to blame if I have failed to understand or heed their advice.

1 Introduction

The purpose of this Element is to set out a theory of price determination in capitalist economies that is consistent with the presumptions of evolutionary analysis. First, an open-system ontology is employed as is essential for evolutionary theorising. Second, prices are determined by the interaction of micro, meso, and macro elements. Third, prices change over time in a process characterised by historical specificity and path dependency. The resulting evolutionary price theory deviates substantively in terms of both construction and implications from neoclassical price theory with its closed-system ontology, methodological individualism, and ahistorical epistemology.

Capitalist economies are open systems that evolve through structural change from within, so evolutionary price theory needs to address how prices facilitate and accommodate structural change and how structural change in turn impacts prices. An undue emphasis on ratiocination in neoclassical theory has extracted a high cost, neglecting imagination and creative vitality. With humans questioning and acting creatively to change their circumstances, prices do more than guide the allocation of scarce resources. They provide information used by entrepreneurs and their financiers in evaluating the profitability of innovations. The dual informational role of prices means the information provided to entrepreneurs can disrupt the order created through coordinating the activities of non-innovating buyers and sellers (Bloch and Metcalfe 2018).

Equilibrium is a closed-system concept that ignores the use of price information by entrepreneurs. Equilibrium according to Schumpeter (1954, p. 969) implies, 'a set of values of the variables that will have no tendency to vary *under the sole influence of the facts included in the relations per se*' [italic in the original]. Reliable information conveyed to entrepreneurs in stable prices combined with their heterogeneous and ever-changing knowledge means such an equilibrium is implausible under capitalism. Schumpeter ([1950] 1976, p. 82) clearly recognises this, noting, 'Capitalism, then, is by nature a form or method of economic change and not only never is but never can be stationary.'

Nelson (2013) suggests using the concept of market order rather than equilibrium in developing an approach to price theory consistent with the open-system perspective of evolutionary economic theory. Nelson argues that for markets not experiencing disruptive innovations a price theory based on market order has subtle, but important, differences from conventional price theory in the treatment of the behaviour of economic agents (behaviour according to routines replaces optimising behaviour) and the outcome of market interaction (order replaces equilibrium). However, for markets affected by disruptive innovations, 'neither the standard conceptions of price theory or the more complex notions of market order presented here may have much use in the analysis of what is going on' (Nelson, 2013, p. 31).

Schumpeter ([1950] 1976) characterises markets undergoing disruptive innovation as subject to creative destruction. Creative destruction is a selection process. Innovation adds to variety in the market. Firms whose innovations pass the test of the market are rewarded with high profits, providing the finance required for them to grow relative to established rivals. The products, processes, and routines of the innovators thereby gradually displace those of established firms. Variation, selection, and retention are all parts of the evolutionary dynamic played out in the institutional context of a market economy.

Evolutionary price theory incorporates the evolutionary dynamic by analysing the interaction of heterogeneous firms, including between innovators and established firms, to explain the time path of adjustment in prices and market shares. Discontinuities and path dependence are inevitable in an error-ridden adjustment process, given decisions made on incomplete information and an unknown future. Structural change at the level of the aggregate economy results from the combination of markets experiencing disruption, which usually constitute only a portion of all markets, and the great bulk of orderly markets in which agents operate according to well-established routines.[1]

Fundamental to evolutionary price theory is the micro-meso-macro framework widely used in evolutionary economic analysis (Dopfer et al. 2004). At the micro level, prices change when the behaviour of consumers and firms change,

---

[1] Mainstream price theory avoids analysing these issues by assuming consumers and firms operate optimally with perfect information. The focus is on market coordination of the activities of these idealised consumers and firms, while ignoring the role of markets in the evolutionary dynamic of innovation, creative destruction, and structural change.

with their creative activity generating new knowledge and passing new information to other agents. At the meso level, differential performance of established and innovative firms leads to differential firm growth in the process of creative destruction, which changes market shares and impacts average prices and the variance of prices over an industry. Prices change at the macro level due to the impact of changes at the micro and meso levels as well as interactions across sectors. There are also influences from monetary and financial institutions. Causation is far from unidirectional.

This Element builds on the incomplete and imperfect sketch of an evolutionary price theory contained in Schumpeter's writings on capitalist development.[2] Nelson and Winter (1982) and Metcalfe (1998) add essential micro and meso ingredients by analysing the impact on price dynamics from differential firm growth and industry development following on from innovation and firm heterogeneity. Metcalfe (2008) and Nelson (2013) argue for replacing Schumpeter's reliance on the concept of equilibrium with that of order for determining market prices. Bloch (2016b, 2018b) suggests that work on the micro, meso, and macro components of evolutionary price theory can be complemented by incorporating ideas from post-Keynesian theory of administered prices and from Sraffa's (1960) analysis of reproduction prices.

This Element has three parts plus introductory and concluding chapters. Part I deals with economic agents (micro level), Part II with markets and industries (meso level), and Part III with the interactions among industries and with the aggregate economy (macro level). The concluding chapter summarises and points to directions for further research.

Part I begins in Chapter 2 with discussion of individual and household behaviour under conditions of imperfect information, limited cognition, and uncertainty that underpin an evolutionary approach to consumer demand. Following in Chapter 3 is a corresponding discussion of firm behaviour, together with discussion of the need for coordination within the firm of individuals with differing knowledge and information. Routine and habitual behaviour by consumers and the use of rules and routines by firms are central to evolutionary analysis of pricing.

Meso-level analysis in Part II focusses on connections and interactions, between buyers and sellers in markets, and among firms in industries. Chapter 4 considers the balancing supply and demand as the condition for order in markets with undifferentiated products and numerous buyers and sellers, while the use of administered prices and maintenance of excess capacity by firms creates order in markets with heterogeneous products or small numbers of suppliers and buyers. Chapter 5 analyses how differential firm growth among

---

[2] Bloch (2018a) outlines and critiques the price theory contained in Schumpeter's work.

heterogeneous firms producing related products leads to changes in industry structure as well as generating dynamics for product prices.

Part III is devoted to analysis of the aggregate price level. Chapter 6 discusses the relationship between firms and industries in the context of restless knowledge, before examining the transmission of prices across industries through input–output relationships. Schumpeter's (1939) argument that the business cycle is due to waves of innovations associated with the changing reliability of price information is then considered in Chapter 7, along with the role of monetary and financial institutions. Chapter 8 concludes with a summary and discussion of directions for further development of evolutionary price theory.

Part I Micro

2 Consumers

Bloch and Metcalfe (2024) observe that the strong rationality postulate underlying much modern economic discourse is increasingly rejected by behavioural economists and complexity theorists (Shiller 2000, Kirman 2011, Arthur 2015). Behaviour is goal directed but calculations need to be made within the confines of limited cognition and present limited knowledge, knowledge that is heterogeneous across individuals and changes by experience and creativity. Bounded rationality and satisficing routines are more reasonable presumptions than optimisation for analysing individual behaviour (Potts 2000, Dopfer et al. 2004, Foster 2005, Earl 2023).

The personal and changing nature of knowledge is widely recognised in the evolutionary analysis of individual and organisational behaviour. Implications for the behaviour of firms have been at the forefront, justifying the replacement of the assumption of optimising behaviour with behaviour according to rules and routines since at least the seminal work of Nelson and Winter (1982). There has also been analysis of the implications for markets and institutions (Loasby 1999, Potts 2001). In this chapter the focus is on the implications for the evolutionary analysis of consumer decision making and demand.

2.1 Knowing and Acting

Heterogeneity of individuals is recognised in mainstream analysis in terms of differentiated preferences for goods and differentiated skills for workers. This heterogeneity is pointed to as justifying a downward slope to consumer demand for individual products and an upward slope of supply for labour with specialised skills, both contribute to rationalising the stability of equilibrium.

However, no heterogeneity is allowed in how individuals make decisions, with every decision being an optimising decision usually based on perfect information or at least rational expectations. Also, whatever heterogeneity of individuals exists is assumed constant for short-run analysis and determined by external influences in long-run analysis.

Imagination is central to the creation of novelty. As Shackle (1959, p. 753) notes, 'in a nondeterministic universe where creation of something essentially new can happen from moment to moment, then the individual imagination seems to be the locus, so far as human beings are concerned, of this continual projection of essential novelty into the world process.' When faced with choice, individuals may respond creatively and act in novel ways.

Human beings are by nature inquisitive and to the extent that they think differently can conjecture different answers to the same question. These different answers transform the state of knowing, such that every solution to a problem has the capacity to define further problems and the growth of human knowing becomes autocatalytic and open. Because individuals know differently, it is not surprising that they behave differently and their behaviour changes over time as their knowledge changes. Loasby (1999, p. 43) highlights the contribution to economic evolution from heterogeneity and continual change in individual knowledge and behaviour,

> What we can reasonably conclude is that the differences between people, partly endogenous, and partly the result of their particular cognitive development, in the patterns of connections by which they make choices or recognise a need for a reconstruction of their strategies for making choices, are primary contributors to the generation of variety and thus to the evolution of economic systems.

Deciding and acting in the presence of uncertainty are problematic in modern economies (Levine 1997). The certainties of traditional society have been removed and replaced with an environment subject to the vagaries of restless knowledge. No matter how carefully we develop knowledge, we may be surprised by an unexpected outcome as most action takes place in an environment of at least partial ignorance. Every action generates new information and potentially leads to a change in knowing. Loasby (1999, p. 149) references Shackle in noting, 'the incompleteness and dispersion of knowledge are a constant source of opportunities for creating new knowledge; as some ambiguities are resolved, more are revealed, and people are inspired to imagine new ways of closing their cognitive systems'.

The occasional discovery and creative action occur against a background of routinised behaviour. Uncertainty, limited cognition, and imperfect information encourage behaviour according to habits or routines. Hodgson (1997) argues habits and rules are ubiquitous in governing individual decisions. Both habits and rules 'have the form in circumstances X, do Y', where 'Rules do not essentially have a self-actuating or autonomous quality but clearly, by repeated application, a rule can become a habit' (Hodgson 1997, p. 664).

Habits and rules are in part based on personal experience, so reflect learning from both expected and unexpected experiences (Witt 2001). They are also partly based on the social and institutional environment in which the individual operates. The role of institutions and society in formation of habits is at the centre of evolutionary theorising about individual and household behaviour by Veblen (1899). An individual acts in accordance with their perceived and desired position in society, leading to patterns of consumption that include conspicuous consumption, bandwagon effects, and snob effects.

Individuals are always constrained by rules of the game governing their freedom to act. In a market economy many informal restraints that shape interaction arise in the context of local interactions, local knowledge, and the specific experience of time and place, leading to geographical and historical specificity. Governments set regulations governing the way market interaction occurs (dispute resolution, quality assurance, health and safety matters for example). These regulations often are responses to experiences generated within the system and change over time, coevolving with the activities they are meant to regulate (Dopfer and Potts 2008).

Routines are at the centre of the evolutionary approach to decision making. Earl (2023, p. 4) reviews the approaches to decision making in old and new behavioural economics as well as evolutionary economics and suggests, 'The evolving sets of rules, heuristics, principles and routines that decision-makers use to deal with the challenges of everyday life may be genetically inherited, personally created or outsourced/absorbed from social networks, society in a wider sense and market institutions.' These sets of decision-making rules are the outcome of a process where, 'Economic evolution entails the creation of new rules and a competitive selection process whereby the relative populations of different rules (or sets of rules) change, with associated changes in the connective architecture of the economic system and of its subsystems' (Earl 2023, p. 3). This conception of decision making underpins much of the evolutionary approach to consumer demand, which is discussed in the next section.

2.2 Consumer Demand

Early contributions to evolutionary analysis of consumer demand attack neoclassical assumptions of optimising behaviour, especially as applied to new goods. Metcalfe (2001) argues optimisation is neither necessary nor useful in analysing consumer behaviour, suggesting the effects of changes in price and incomes can be well handled by focussing on the time and budget constraints facing consumers in a way that also allows analysis of the demand for new goods. Witt (2001) notes the role of the evolution of consumers wants in explaining the avoidance of satiation despite the enormous growth of personal consumption under modern capitalism.

Despite this early work, Nelson and Consoli (2010) lament the absence of a modern evolutionary theory of household consumption behaviour. They then sketch the outlines of such an evolutionary theory, starting with the requirement that individual rationality is bounded. Households are viewed as engaging in activities to satisfy their wants subject to constraints of income and time, with the degree of success depending on the household's ability to effectively coordinate its activities. Learning is important to improving this ability, meaning 'consumption decisions need to be recognized as largely a matter of routine plus marginal changes in routine, except when the household is facing circumstances that are significantly new to it' (Nelson and Consoli 2010, p. 678). Learning is particularly important in the context of new goods and services, 'the response of households to the availability of new goods and services may involve a significant reorientation of their targets and goals, which in many cases only can be accomplished in the course of learning to do new things' (Nelson and Consoli 2010, p. 681–682).

Chai and Babutsidze (2024) review the substantial body of work that has been done since Nelson and Consoli (2010) to fill gaps in evolutionary consumer theory. Notable advances have occurred, including in the modelling of bounded rationality, understanding the impact of innovation in consumer goods on escaping the satiation trap implied by Engel Curves relating consumption expenditure to income, and the role of social networks in the diffusion of new goods. Chai and Babutsidze (2024, p. 270) conclude, 'This body of work has contributed to developing a more realistic understanding of i) consumer decision-making, ii) the process of preference formation, iii) the role of consumers in the innovation process, iv) the diffusion of innovations among heterogenous consumers and v) the co-evolution of demand and supply.'

For long-period analysis, treating consumer preferences as exogenous, as in neoclassical theory, is not useful. Consumer preferences are impacted by structural change in the economy as well changes in demographics, culture, and politics. For example, current real wages affect housing status, family formation, and population growth, which in turn affect the future age structure of the population, labour force, output, and consumer demand.[3]

Consumer demand needs to be considered as part of the coevolutionary process involving the economy and all other aspects of society, including the process of change in economic, cultural, educational, and political institutions (Dopfer and Potts 2008, Almudi et al. 2021). Potts (2017) points to the coevolution of institutions and consumer demand in explaining why Keynes (1930) was so wildly wrong in his prediction regarding the expansion in leisure that would accompany growth in productive capacity over time. Potts argues Keynes ignored innovation under capitalism is endogenous and is oriented towards generating profit, which means a bias towards encouraging production and consumption of new goods over pure leisure. Expanding production under capitalism cannot solve the economic problem of scarcity because creating markets (and the preferences underlying demand) attracts the attention of entrepreneurs.

Time is required for novel products to build up a substantial market. Earl (2022, Chapter 11.7) refers to the uptake of novel products as following a meso trajectory, with the number of users of a novel product increasing over time along an S-shaped curve. In the origination phase, the novel product attracts a niche market of pioneering buyers who have a particular interest in the distinguishing features of the novel product, and who learn about the product through their social networks or other specialist sources. Initially, the product is often expensive relative to available alternatives, and to its own future price, due to high start-up production cost.

Earl (2022, Chapter 11.9) cites several barriers to the rapid adoption of new technology, including the high initial cost to the consumer, the uncertainty regarding the success of competing standards for the new technology (as in Betamax versus VHS for video players), and limited availability of complementary products (as in the limited proportion of all music available on CDs). As prices of the new technology fall, technological standards are clarified, and availability of complements expands as more consumers are attracted. Eventually, new lifestyles evolve incorporating the novel product, as has been the case of with household appliances, including washing machines, dishwashers, and air conditioners. Suburban lifestyles based on the automobile with

---

[3] Classical economists (Smith [1776] 1937, Malthus [1798] 1991, Ricardo [1821] 1973) clearly recognised this interdependence in specifying that the natural wage of labour is determined by the subsistence requirements of a worker and their family. Neoclassical economics ignores this long-run sustainability condition, instead treating the size, composition, and needs of the population as exogenously determined.

shopping centres and long distances to work provide an excellent example of the coevolution of novel products and institutions.

When novel products reach the maturity phase of the meso trajectory, they have been acquired by very large proportions of the target population. In the case of durable products, new sales depend on replacement demand. Marketing efforts switch to convincing consumers to replace their current model with something new and better, while for nondurables the effort is on increasing the quantity consumed by each consumer. Saturation of the market limits the growth of demand, with the novel product having reached the top of the S-shaped diffusion curve.

Where does the discussion of this section leave an evolutionary theory of consumer demand? The mainstream assumption of unlimited calculation ability and perfect information are clearly rejected. The notion that buyers always can identify and transact at the best available offer is unviable. Their purchases are subject to the incomplete distribution of information on prices and product availability, introducing a stochastic element into the amount bought at any price. Yet, as Nelson and Consoli (2010, p. 679) point out, 'the "demand curves" described here are capable of doing many of the same jobs as the demand curves depicted and rationalized in neoclassical theory.'

Differences between the 'demand curves' of evolutionary theory and those of neoclassical theory are generally a matter of degree, at least for goods and services for which consumers have established routines. Constraints on information and decision-making ability encourage reliance on habits and routines that lead to inertia in consumer behaviour. Consequences include limited response to changes in income and prices as compared to optimising behaviour, especially in the very short run. Hence, the short-run price elasticity of demand for mature consumer goods and services is likely to be low. Likewise, the short-run marginal propensity to consume out of income is expected to be below the corresponding average propensity. Over time, greater adjustment occurs, better understood as a lagged response than a higher long-run elasticity, as path dependency means adjustments continue even if the price or income change is reversed.

Foster (2021) uses the evolutionary approach outlined earlier to develop a model of aggregate consumption building on the Keynesian approach of Dusenberry (1949). Aggregate consumption has two components. The first component 'is determined by a precommitment to a particular set of interconnected behavioural rules, ranging from meso-rules that are broad and cultural, down to personal commitments to individual routines and habits that are influenced by targeted advertising and marketing' (Foster 2021, p. 783). This component accounts for the bulk of consumption expenditure and is heavily path dependent, so current aggregate consumption depends heavily on past consumption. The second component consists of purchases of novel goods and services and follows a diffusion process as awareness and interest in these novelties spread through networks. Diffusion builds the impact of expanding connections into aggregate consumption through networks of individuals, with limits set by the size of the relevant population.

Foster estimates parameters of the model with data from the US economy from 1972 to 2018. The results are consistent with the hypothesised relationship and suggest a gradually waning impact of consumerism, which is the dominant meso-rule stimulating consumer demand for novelties since the middle of the twentieth century. As a result, the impact of fiscal policy on growth is weaker than in earlier decades and greater expansions of money or budget-financed credit are required to keep unemployment low.

2.3 Conclusions

The mainstream characterisation of the representative consumer maximising utility with exogenously determined preferences is unhelpful, even destructive to understanding economic evolution. Individuals are heterogeneous, with differentiated knowledge, cultures, and experiences. They have imperfect information and limited cognition, which leads to reliance on habits and routines in decision-making. They are also occasionally creative, especially in dealing with disappointed expectations, novel circumstances, and new products.

Consumer demand reflects the use of routines and habits to deal with imperfect information and limited cognition in a changing and uncertain environment. Demand takes time to adjust to changes in price or income, while demand for new products depends on diffusion of interest through networks of individuals. Evolutionary analysis resolves the satiation problem, as demand coevolves with the supply of novel products in an unending process moulded by institutional frameworks and social networks.

3 Firms

Optimisation is rejected as a principle governing decision making at firms in critiques of the mainstream theory of the firm by Cyert and March (1963), Simon (1964), and Shackle (1970). For evolutionary analysis, optimisation is inconsistent with emergence and complexity, which are fundamental properties of an evolving economy. In a review of theories and empirics on firm growth, Coad (2009, p. 8) argues, contrary to neoclassical economics, 'firms are not rational, many fail, and that many miss opportunities. Furthermore, many firms may shape their own destinies, as it were, and make opportunities for themselves that did not seem to exist before.' For purposes of evolutionary price theory, firm behaviour is assumed to be governed by rules and routines developed over the unique historical experience the firm, which reflects the connections among individuals with specialised knowledge internal and external to the firm.

Mainstream economics treats all firms operating within an industry as identical. No other outcome is logically possible given the assumptions of universally optimising behaviour with perfect information and equal access to technology and markets. Winter (2006) points out history, dynamics, and probability combine to ensure firms differ. Firms exist in the modern economy in a bewildering variety of sizes, scope of operations, forms of governance, and orientations.

For purposes of developing an evolutionary price theory, three aspects of the differences among firms are discussed. First are the related characteristics of the size, scope, and organisation of the firm, with small, large and mega-firms distinguished. Second, different goal orientations of firms are surveyed, with profit, growth, and innovation discussed. Finally, the relation between the firm and the market is considered, distinguishing between price-taker and price-maker firms. The chapter closes with an illustration of application of evolutionary price theory for the case of a novel product that has no close competitors. Price theory for markets with multiple sellers is presented in subsequent chapters, orderly markets in Chapter 4, and disrupted markets in Chapter 5.[4]

3.1 Firm Size, Scope, and Organisation

A better understanding of the variety of behaviour across firms can be achieved by distinguishing categories of firms according to size, scope, and organisation. Firm size is important as only larger firms can internally reap full advantages of specialisation from the division of labour. However, specialisation within the firm poses challenges of coordination and resistance to innovation. These challenges increase with the scope of firm activities, but increased scope offers opportunities for diversification and synergy, especially in relation to innovation through new products, processes, and markets.

3.1.1 Small Firms

Most firms are small in terms of sales and employment, privately owned, and produce a limited range of products serving a narrow range of customer needs. The traditional terminology of family-owned firm fits well in conveying that the

---

[4] Topics of the choice of technique and the relationship between output and cost are overlooked in this chapter as they are well covered in mainstream texts. These topics are relevant to evolutionary price theory, but not as central as to mainstream analysis with its emphasis on marginal cost. The measure of production cost that matters in evolutionary price theory is average cost, especially average variable cost, as explained in Section 3.3.2.

cognition and communication issues for these firms overlap those facing individuals and households discussed in the last chapter. However, the production activity of the small firm tends to be highly specialised to take advantage of the gains from specialised expertise. Specialisation combines with idiosyncratic skills, experience, and information of owners to ensure there is substantial variety in performance among the group of small firms producing any commodity. Small firms dominate parts of the supply of personal services (hair salons and massage parlours) as well as household services (electricians and plumbers). They have dominated many retail businesses, such as groceries, bakeries, restaurants, and hotels, but these businesses are increasingly dominated by chain or franchise operations. They have also dominated agricultural production, and still do in many parts of the world.

Marshall (1920, p. 263–264) suggests the growth of the family-owned firm is limited by the vitality of its founder, 'Nature still presses on the private business by limiting the life of its original founders, and by limiting even more narrowly that part of their lives in which their faculties retain full vigour.' He then uses the analogy of trees in a forest to discuss the diverse experience of growing and declining firms producing a commodity, suggesting the need to focus on a representative firm when analysing activity for the whole industry.

Activity of the small firm is not only limited by the life span and vitality of the founder. Personal wealth typically places a constraint on the size of the family-owned firm, much as income places a constraint on the consumption of the household (Steindl 1945). Borrowing is possible but only in amounts limited by Kalecki's (1937) principle of increasing risk. Also, as noted in the last chapter, the knowledge and skill of individuals are generally limited, meaning the scope of activity in which the small firm is competitive is restricted. Adding employees to successfully provide for expansion requires additional skills in management. Not surprisingly, most firms remain small even if they manage to survive more than a few years.

Profit is a typical objective of the small firm, as the income of the owner depends on it. Survival is also front of mind, with minimal buffers available to deal with unexpected shocks and limited access to external finance. If the firm is successful and generates unexpected profits, there is a tendency to reinvest these profits in the same activities given that the financial constraint to expansion has been relaxed and the market has responded favourably to the firm.

3.1.2 Large Firms

Among the few firms that discover longevity, a very small number grow to a large size and scope. Size and scope challenge the capabilities of a family-owned firm, leading to institutional change. Recognition of the development of a different species of firm is certainly not new, with roots at least as far back as Marshall's (1920) treatment of joint-stock companies. Such companies were common in undertaking large projects, such as building canals and railways in the eighteenth and nineteenth centuries. By the early twentieth century large enterprises had come to dominate large swathes of industry in the United States and Europe. For example, Ford Motors in automobiles, US Steel in steel making, and Standard Oil in petroleum refining.

The distinctive organisational and behavioural characteristics of modern large corporations are discussed in *The Modern Corporation and Private Property* (Berle and Means 1932). Subsequent theoretical contributions build on the separation of ownership and control identified by Berle and Means. Managerial objectives, other than profit maximisation, are identified as drivers of decision making by Baumol (1958), Marris (1964), Wood (1975), and Eichner (1976).

Large organisations can benefit from specialisation, with individuals developing expertise in dealing with small sets of tasks. However, to function effectively, separate individuals, teams and departments within the organisation must coordinate their specialised knowledge. Development of methods for ensuring internal coordination is itself a specialised task and the subject of specialised study since, at least the work of Taylor (1911), Marshall (1923, especially Chapter 11), and Barnard (1966 [1938]).

Knowledge is a state of the individual mind. A large firm depends on a degree of correlation of the knowledge of team members, that they understand their tasks in common, that when asked a question or confronted by a command they act in very similar, typically indistinguishable, ways. Correlated behaviour is routinised behaviour, reliable behaviour that is confidently shared. The degree of sharing is highly uneven, depending on the context. At one level it may involve knowledge shared with very few others, but by degrees of generalisation we find kinds of knowing shared across the business department or the whole firm, albeit at a conceptual rather than practical level.

How is the necessary correlation of knowledge in large firms brought about? Knowledge is a state of mind that is necessarily inseparable from the person who knows. Information, by contrast, is an expression in some form of what the individual knows, it is not knowledge per se, but rather a particular representation of that knowing. Information is a public representation of private knowing, so information is inherently incomplete. Direct communication between employees allows communication going beyond codified information. The large firm has a distinct advantage as information and communication requirements can be economised through appropriately designed organisational structure (Arrow 1974).

Firms differ because each employee imagines differently, and because the interaction and coordination between employees is organised differently. What employees imagine differs because they are different individuals, bringing different expertise and experience to understand phenomena and to develop their understandings. The firm's unique manner of organisation further differentiates the learning process because of differences in the manner of learning across firms. New imaginings are constantly being added and diffused within the firm, whereas old imaginings are forgotten or even rejected. Without such dynamics of individual knowledge within the firm it is impossible for the firm to change endogenously, impossible to conceive of innovation, which necessarily differentiates firms.

Mainstream theory of the firm assumes given technology, products and market demand and factor supply conditions that constrain behaviour. Optimisation under these constraints is then imposed for analysing the comparative statics of the impact of exogenous changes in technology and factor supply conditions. No consideration is given to how firms might develop from within, how they develop endogenously and deliberatively.[5]

3.1.3 Mega-firms

An organisational development in large firms is the emergence of mega-firms discussed by Bloch and Metcalfe (2015). Mega-firms constitute a sub-species of large firms, which are particularly well suited to dealing with the evolutionary context of the modern economy. In Bloch and Metcalfe emphasis is placed on the role of the internal structure and external linkages of mega-firms in the innovation process, shifting focus from the market as a selection mechanism that features in much neo-Schumpeterian literature. Mega-firms have considerable protection from markets, including capital markets, through their large size and scope, which provides them with the ability to internally generate and allocate resources for growth, diversification, and innovation. An early example of a mega-firm is General Electric that diversified from light globes to electronic equipment to jet engines and the financing thereof. A more recent example, Amazon has moved from online book sales to a generalised online marketplace as well as cloud computing services.

---

[5] As discussed in more detail in Chapter 6, Penrose (1959) bases a theory of the growth of firms on the limits to growth posed by the need to develop extra managerial resources through diversion of the effort of existing managers. Penrose's approach has been further developed in the literature on dynamic capabilities and the resource-based view of the firm (Barney 1991, Dosi, et al. 2002 and Teece 2009).

Mega-firms are complex organisational systems, produce many goods or services, often in different geographical locations, sell in different kinds of markets to customers who put their goods and services to different uses, and purchase many kinds of input to support their production activities. Employees of the firm are individually knowledgeable, but their knowledge is highly circumscribed and pertinent to a narrow aspect of the firm's functioning. They are ignorant with respect to the totality of knowledge deployed by the mega-firm. Winter (2006, p. 135) identifies the fundamental difficulty facing such firms in question-and-answer format,

> Does anybody in the large firm know what's going on? Answer: No. Any single individual's conceptual understanding of the firm in its entirety is mainly at an extremely abstract and aggregative level. Knowledge representing many lifetimes of education, training and experience is represented in such a conceptual picture by a few names of occupations and organizational subunits.

How the mega-firm operates then depends on how pools of localised knowledge are connected. Shared understanding among individuals with specialised knowledge contributes to the cohesion, and hence, stability of the mega-firm. However, shared understanding is undermined by the ongoing learning in separate parts of the organisation. A tension exists between the standardisation of practices into routines that underpin the shared understanding and efficiency of the mega-firm and the quite different practices required for change. Leadership in the form of entrepreneurship is required to overcome this tension, so the mega-firm is an entrepreneurial firm.

Mega-firms have a competitive advantage from the extensive capabilities and specialised knowledge of large numbers of individuals, which allows them to reap dynamic economies through the coordination of a division of labour. Importantly, mega-firm capabilities expand organically from the interaction of the knowledge of individuals, enhanced by introspection and creative problem solving, which provides some protection for the firm against the ravages of creative destruction in the competitive process. To put this in the language of business strategy, mega-firms are organised to achieve sustainable competitive advantage (Porter 1985).

3.2 Orientations of Firms

Evolutionary economics is history friendly. Path dependency, historical events, and individual personalities feature prominently in the accounts of the development of individual firms and industries (Chandler 1962 and 1977, Malerba et al. 1999, Dopfer 2001). The observed variety of firms in the economy reflects the importance of their separate experiences. It also reflects the different ways in which firms interact with their environment. In this section, four orientations of firms are discussed, survival, profit, growth, and innovation. A firm may have multiple orientations, which are often complementary as noted at points in the discussion next.

3.2.1 Survival

Survival is a precondition to the pursuit of any other objective by a firm. Mainstream economics with its assumptions of perfect information and rational expectations ignores the early death experienced by most firms. When the environment is only partially known and continually changing in unexpected ways, mistakes are made and often fatal. Unrealistic assessments of firm capabilities are also common. A firm's life is typically precarious and short.

Firms can act to reduce exposure to risk. For example, reducing borrowing and other long-run financial commitments means a lower probability that a future unexpected downturn in revenues or increase in costs leave the firm exposed to insolvency. However, hazards associated with uncertainty, the unknowable aspects of the future in an evolving economy, are unavoidable (Knight [1921] 1971).

Choosing a strategy to achieve survival in an evolving economy is not straightforward. A strategy of sticking with established routines is not foolproof. Witness the fate of established firms who don't imitate or innovate when faced with Schumpeter's perennial gale of creative destruction. Survival requires alertness to changes in economic environment and appropriate responses. There is no guarantee of success, but it is reasonable to expect firms with a survival orientation to be over-represented in the population of surviving firms.

3.2.2 Profit

Profit maximisation is not a realistic objective, but an orientation towards profit has benefits for firms. Profit is the source of personal wealth for family-owned firms. Profit is positively linked to share price for publicly traded corporations, which impacts performance appraisal and bonuses of managers as well as on the value of their share options.

As well as being directly desirable, profit can be the means to an end. The connection between profit and survival is clear when unpredictable shocks are an unavoidable part of doing business. Profit also is important in the pursuit of growth or innovation.

In mainstream analysis of a world of perfect information and rational expectations, financing growth of production capacity or research and development activities aimed at innovation is straightforward. Determining the profits from investments in growth or innovation is simply a matter of calculation, available to a firm and to its financial backers. However, as explained in Section 5.1.2, the situation is radically different in an evolving economy with incomplete information, limited cognition, and an unknowable future. Realised profits enable risky investments in growth and innovation by providing a market test of success for potential backers as well as a direct means of finance.

3.2.3 Growth

Growth features as an objective for firm behaviour in some mainstream and post-Keynesian theory of the firm as discussed in the section earlier. A preference for growth over profit is linked to the separation of managerial control from ownership. Managers benefit from overseeing larger operations in terms of power, prestige, and salary. Growth and large size also help protect managers against losing control through merger or acquisition.

From an evolutionary perspective, growth is an obvious orientation to attribute to firms. Metcalfe (1998, p. 29) suggests, 'an evolutionary process explains how population structures change over time, and how structure is an emergent property.' Under capitalism, innovations are spread in good part through the relative growth of innovating firms. Faster growth of innovating firms than their non-innovating rivals diffuses the innovation, increasing the share of output carrying the innovation. An orientation towards growth for innovating firms thus facilitates the evolutionary process.

3.2.4 Innovation

Schumpeter (1961 [1934]) assigns a special role, entrepreneurship, to the initiator of innovation and associates this role with the founding of new firms. These firms are small and individually controlled. While he later shifts focus to the role of large industrial firms as sources of innovation (Schumpeter 1976 [1950]), observation suggests small firms remain prominent as sources of innovation in modern economies (Acs and Audretsch 1988).

Schumpeter points to the need for leadership to overcome resistance to change and divert means of production from established activities to new uses. Overcoming resistance to change for a small firm generally involves resistance in the external environment. If obtaining means of production requires finance beyond the personal wealth of the owner or immediate family, banks or other external backers need to be convinced of the merits of the innovation. Only few small firms are likely to be led by individuals with the requisite skills.

For the large firm, resistance is likely to be within the organisation. Large firms may reallocate means of production from other activities or use existing lines of finance, but only when the competing interests within the firm can be overcome and the directors are convinced that the innovation has merit. Innovation is problematic in large firms because of the tension between the routines that underpin the efficiency of the firm and the different routines required for change. The former depends upon shared understanding within the firm as to its routines, whereas the latter depends on challenging and breaking the rigidity associated with the pursuit of efficiency. The former is the domain of management in a narrow sense, while the latter is the domain of entrepreneurial imagination, of thinking through how the firm could be different with respect to activity and organisation. Some, but not all, large firms are organised to overcome internal resistance and develop an orientation towards innovation.

The mega-firm with its large size and scope is well suited to resolve the tension between efficiency and innovation by devoting efforts to the integration of new knowledge within the firm. These efforts mean the mega-firm can use its existing capabilities to be able to innovate and to adapt to changing external conditions. Innovation based on connecting knowledge of individuals within a large and complex organisation can point in radically new directions, if supported by the firm's leadership. Thus, the mega-firm fits well with Eliasson's (2024) depiction of the experimentally organised decision team that not only innovates but often operates at the meso level creating new products, processes and, even, new markets, so it is unlikely to be fully identified with only one industry or sector of a single economy, at least not indefinitely.

Innovating firms are problematic for mainstream economic analysis. The explanation of firm behaviour in terms of optimisation subject to constraints is undermined by the self-transforming nature of the innovating firm, which weakens external constraints of technology, resources, and preferences. Optimisation is a dubious assumption for explaining behaviour of any firm in an evolving economy with imperfect information, incomplete networks, and fundamental uncertainty about the future.

Even evolutionary economic analysis is challenged by innovating firms. The boundaries of firms, market and industries are under continual challenge by innovation (Bloch and Finch 2010). However, for analytical purposes it is sometimes useful to associate firms with a particular product, a group of products with a market, or a group of firms with an industry. Examples include the analysis of price as a coordinating mechanism for buyers and sellers in a market (Chapter 4), and the analysis price dynamics as emerging from the selection process among the population of firms in an industry (Chapter 5). Detailed discussion of broader implications for evolutionary price theory of self-transformation by firms is postponed to Chapter 6.

3.3 Pricing Behaviour

Mainstream economics portrays competition as a structural characteristic of markets determined by the number and relative size of buyers and sellers. This is highly misleading, ignoring the roles of technology, institutions, and history in determining patterns of competition. Small firms often operate in a niche market with limited competition, such as the local bakery or a highly specialised professional service provider. Also, very large firms operating in markets for standardised commodities often have very limited control over the current market price of their product, with examples including firms buying and selling commodities like wheat or coal on world markets.

All firms in an evolving economy regardless of size, scope, and organisation face an environment characterised by imperfect information and uncertainty. They also generally operate with a limited number of direct competitors. Crucially, the historical and institutional characteristics of the market are critical in creating the competitive conditions faced by a firm, more so than the number or size distribution of firms emphasised in mainstream economics. Nonetheless, the distinction between price-taker and price-maker firms that features in mainstream theory of perfect and imperfect competition can be usefully adapted to evolutionary price theory.

3.3.1 Price-Taker Firms

Some firms enter the market with a minimum acceptable price and a willingness to sell up to a maximum quantity at or above that price, perhaps with a willingness to expand the quantity sold at higher prices. I categorise these firms in the extreme case as price takers. Though they need not face a horizontal demand curve for their products as in neoclassical price theory, an essential behavioural characteristic is that they don't adjust the quantity supplied to market with the aim of influencing the market price.

In the evolutionary version of price-taker behaviour, firms adapt to the market rather than control it. Nelson (2013) uses this characterisation in discussing how conventional supply and demand analysis can be adapted for evolutionary analysis. Being able to specify minimum price and maximum quantity combinations for each individual buyer or seller, without reference to offers and bids from other market participants, means the quantity bid for or offered at any price can be added together to obtain a market demand or supply curve, respectively. Nelson argues the appropriate balancing concept from an evolutionary perspective is market order rather than market equilibrium. Determination of price in orderly markets is explored in detail in the next chapter.

Institutions and history matter crucially in creating market conditions favourable to price-taker behaviour. Organised commodity markets, such as the Chicago Board of Trade and the London Metals Exchange, are institutional exemplars. Rules and regulations developed over time facilitate the determination of a price balancing bids and offers for a specific variety of commodity at a specified place and word quality. For current and, often, multiple future delivery dates. Historical discounts and premiums then guide price determination for related varieties for other places and word, qualities.

Organised national or international exchanges exist for many of the most important metal and storable agricultural commodities. Perishable agricultural commodities tend to be traded on local auction markets, although government intervention to control marketing is not uncommon. In general, historical development or government design has created market conditions where individual producers of primary commodities are price takers, even when collectively operating as price makers, such as with local marketing boards or, most notably, the Organization of Petroleum Exporting Countries.

Kalecki (1971) examines price formation in modern capitalist economies by associating price-taker behaviour with firms operating in primary production, while manufacturing firms using primary products as raw materials engage in price-maker behaviour. The dichotomy in pricing behaviour means the ratio of the price of raw materials to the price of manufactured goods moves in the same direction as the rate of growth of output over the business cycle. This dichotomy is applied in Chapter 7 to examining the impact of waves of innovation on the price system and the price level.

3.3.2 Price-Maker Firms

Price-maker firms use rules or routines to set a fixed price for each of their products and offer all their available supply at those prices. Prices set by these firms are indirectly impacted by influences of buyer demand for the products or the pricing behaviour of firms selling substitute products. The indirect impact on rules and routines used in pricing is explained in the remainder of this section.[6]

---

[6] The categories price-taker and price-maker aren't exhaustive or necessarily mutually exclusive. Some prices are set through negotiation or through tender processes, and some firms may not have the same pricing practices for all products. These complications are ignored in this Element.

Bloch (2018b) suggests using post-Keynesian pricing rules in developing micro-level analysis for an evolutionary theory of price determination. Post-Keynesian pricing rules are designed to capture the behavioural routines used by firms possessing market power, especially firms that dominate manufacturing in the modern economy. Large and complex enterprises need behavioural routines that can be applied across the organisation and monitored centrally. Importantly, post-Keynesian pricing rules share the presumptions of evolutionary analysis, namely imperfect information, distributed knowledge, open systems, and development from within.

A general characterisation of post-Keynesian pricing rules is that firms set price equal to a measure of normal unit cost multiplied by the firm's desired price-cost ratio (Lee 1999, Bloch 2016b). Normal unit cost is the level of cost when the firm operates at its expected level of capacity utilisation, which is generally well below maximum possible production. Excess capacity provides a buffer for supplying unexpected increases in demand and a strategic deterrent against existing and potential rivals. In some post-Keynesian pricing rules, the measure of unit cost covers the normal full cost of production, including overheads and an allowance for the depreciation of fixed capital. In other variants only labour, raw materials, and intermediate inputs used in current production are included, providing a measure of normal average variable cost. A feature common to all variants is that the measure of normal unit cost doesn't change as output fluctuates in the short period.

Various explanations are given regarding how the price-cost ratio desired by firms is determined. The full-cost pricing rule of Hall and Hitch (1939) emphasises dealing with uncertainty and maintaining long-run sustainability. Monopoly power features prominently in the theoretical work of Kalecki (1971) on mark-up pricing, with the concept of monopoly power extending beyond the market structure notion of neoclassical economics (Kreisler 1987). Requirements for internal financing of firm investment in extra capacity feature in the work of Eichner (1976), Harcourt and Kenyon (1976), and Wood (1975). Steindl (1976) and Sylos-Labini (1962) emphasise the rate of growth of industry demand as well as conditions of entry and exit for the industry in which the firm operates.

A general form of post-Keynesian pricing rules has normal unit cost and the desired price-cost ratio as the proximate determinants of the administered price set by price-maker firms in the short period. The price for the kth firm operating in the ith industry at time t, $p_{k,i,t}$, is given by the firm's normal unit cost, $u_{k,i,t}$, multiplied by the desired price-cost ratio, $\pi_{k,i,t}$,

$$p_{k,i,t} = u_{k,i,t} * \pi_{k,i,t} \tag{3.1}$$

Fluctuations in output due to rising or falling demand have no immediate impact on the desired price-cost ratio or normal unit cost, so the short-period price is unaffected by demand fluctuations. In contrast, changes in prices for intermediate inputs and labour, unless temporary and expected to be reversed, lead to changes in normal unit cost and proportional changes in product price to maintain the desired price-cost ratio.

Key questions in applying post-Keynesian pricing rules to an evolutionary context are what determine the values of normal unit cost and the desired price-cost ratio both at a point in time and in terms of movement over time. Bloch (2016b) addresses these questions in the context of providing a Schumpeterian twist to post-Keynesian price theory. Key issues identified there are whether the costs of overhead and depreciation are included in the unit cost measure or in the desired price-cost ratio, the role of market structure in determination of the desired price-cost ratio, the impact of creative destruction on the dynamics of industry-average values of normal unit cost and desired price-cost ratio, and how obsolescence and R&D costs are handled. These issues are discussed at various points in the following chapters.

3.3.3 Price Leadership

Price-taker and price-maker firms can coexist in the same market. Indeed, models of price leadership presume such coexistence. In the simplest case of price leadership, firms produce virtually identical products and prices for all firms are equal. A single dominant firm, the leader, is the price maker and other firms, followers, act as price takers. Heterogeneity in normal unit cost across firms is accommodated through compensating differentials in price-cost ratios. The price-cost ratio for each of the price-follower firms is determined by its own normal unit cost and the price set by the leading firm, firm d,

$$\pi_{k,i,t} = p_{d,i,t}/u_{k,i,t}, \text{ for } k \neq d \text{ and } p_{d,i,t} = u_{d,i,t} * \pi_{d,i,t} \tag{3.2}$$

Price leadership is an extreme case of interdependence of pricing rules across firms producing similar products. Kalecki (1971, Chapter 5) proposes a pricing rule with a firm's price as a linear function of its own normal unit cost and the average price of related products,

$$p_{k,i,t} = (m_{k,i,t} * u_{k,i,t}) + n_{k,i,t} * \left(\sum_k s_{k,i,t} * p_{k,i,t} \right), m_{k,i,t} \geq 0, n_{k,i,t} \leq 1 \tag{3.3}$$

The last term on the right-hand-side of Equation (3.3) is the weighted average price of all firms producing similar products, with $s_{k,i,t}$ being the share of industry sales accounted for by the kth firm. A greater weight on own cost suggests greater independence in pricing and a greater weight on average price suggests greater interdependence. In the limiting case of price leadership, $m_{jk,i,t} > 1$ and $n_{k,i,t} = 0$ for the price leader, while $m_{k,i,t} = 0$ and $n_{k,i,t} = 1$ for price followers (Asimakopoulos 1975, Bloch 1990).

The firm's price increases with both the $m_{k,i,t}$ and $n_{k,i,t}$ coefficients, given levels of its own unit cost and the average price of similar products. These pricing coefficients can vary over firms, with the price leadership case being an extreme example. The average price across all firms is given by,

$$\bar{p}_{i,t} = \left[\bar{m}_{i,t}/(1 - \bar{n}_{i,t})\right]\bar{u}_{i,t} \tag{3.4}$$

where a bar over a variable or coefficient indicates it is an appropriately weighted average over the group of products as with average price in the last term of (3.3). Kalecki (1971, Chapter 5) refers to the term $\left[\bar{m}_{i,t}/(1 - \bar{n}_{i,t})\right]$ as the degree of monopoly for the industry consisting of the group of producers. The degree of monopoly is influenced by a range of factors, including industry concentration, the degree of sales promotion, overhead costs as a proportion of total costs, and the strength of trade unions.[7]

The expressions in (3.3) and (3.4) are useful in evolutionary price theory because they connect individual firm price setting to the firm's own normal unit cost and the average price in the industry. Innovation by a single firm impacts its cost and price, which then flows through to the prices of other firms in the industry. Average price for the industry is determined by the averages of pricing coefficients and unit cost across all the firms in the industry, which means that average price changes with the distribution of market shares as well as changes in pricing coefficients and normal unit cost at individual firms. Changing structure of market shares due to differential firm growth is at the centre of analysing price dynamics for markets disrupted by innovation in Chapter 5.

3.3.4 Pricing of Novel Products

Novel products are central to the evolutionary process. Distinctive new products feature prominently in consumer expenditures over the modern era, products such as computers and mobile phones most recently, adding to televisions and

---

[7] Kalecki's explanation of the degree of monopoly is critically discussed in Kriesler (1987) and Downward (1999).

air conditioners for the previous generation, automobiles and radios for the generation before, and the even earlier mass production of textiles, clothing, and footwear. Such products have been essential in maintaining consumption as a share of household income despite rising real incomes noted by Foster (2021) as discussed in Chapter 2.

Novel producer products have been essential for transforming production processes. Mechanised assembly lines, electrification, computers, and robots are among the array of novel products raising labour productivity and lowering manufacturing costs. Railroads, trucks, planes, and fossil-fuel powered ships have connected manufacturers to cheaper sources of raw materials and intermediate products. In primary production, costs have been dramatically reduced and output increased using novel products such as tractors, synthetic fertilisers, seismic mapping, dredge lines, computers, and drones.

Pricing of novel products is complicated. The producer faces great uncertainty regarding buyer reaction and the cost of production over the full meso trajectory of origination, adoption and retention for the product as discussed in Chapter 2. Mainstream economics ignores the issue. Novelty is inconsistent with the certainty presumed in perfectly competitive equilibrium.

Pricing analysis discussed in previous sections is compatible with novel products, but a nuanced and multi-phase application is required. Nuance is required in combining elements of the analysis of price takers, price makers, and price leadership. Further, separate analyses are required for each phase of the meso trajectory of origination, adoption, and retention of the novel product.

Initially, the producer of the novel product is a price maker without close competitors, but its circumstances differ from those of an established seller who is a monopolist. In particular, the producer of the novel product can take the prices of its distant competitors as given because it looms small as a threat when its product is first introduced. In this sense, the firm starts in a situation with somewhat like a follower firm under conditions of price leadership.

In its situation as a price follower, the prices of established products provide benchmarks for the producer of the novel product. For consumer goods, the buyer needs to fit the novel product into the established pattern of expenditure. Comparisons to existing products that satisfy related wants are inevitable, with price as well as product characteristics evaluated in terms of value for money. For producer goods, the novel product is attractive when the downstream producer can lower its production cost. The price of currently purchased producer goods determines the comparison cost.

Pricing novel products using an adapted version of Kalecki's model of price-setting equation, (3.3), includes a benchmarking role for prices of established firms. The price of the novel product of an entrepreneurial firm, e, that starts a new industry, n, is given by,

$$p_{e,n,t} = (m_{e,n,t} * u_{e,n,t}) + n_{e,n,t} * \bar{p}_{c,t}, \text{ where } n_{e,n,t} > 0 \text{ and}$$
$$\bar{p}_{c,t} = \left(\sum_i \sum_k s_{k,i,t} * p_{k,i,t}\right) \quad (3.5)$$

Weights used in calculating the average price of competing products, $\bar{p}_{c,t}$, are shares of prospective customers for the novel product who are currently buying products of other firms scattered across established industries. Each competing price is scaled to a quantity equivalent to a unit of the novel product. The value of the parameter, $n_{e,n,t}$, is determined based on the competing needs of the entrepreneur for a high price to generate profits to finance growth in productive capacity and for a low price to attract customers from competitors.

In the origination phase of the meso trajectory of a novel product is viable only if its price exceeds it unit cost. If $m_{e,n,t}$ is set equal to one and both sides of (3.5) are divided by unit direct cost of the novel product, the resulting equation for determining the product's price-cost ratio is,

$$p_{e,n,t}/u_{e,n,t} = 1 + n_{e,n,t} * (\bar{p}_{c,t}/u_{e,n,t}) \quad (3.6)$$

The novel product is a value proposition to customers of competing products when,

$$\bar{p}_{c,t}/p_{e,n,t} = (\bar{p}_{c,t}/u_{e,n,t})/(p_{e,n,t}/u_{e,n,t}) > 1 \quad (3.7)$$

This occurs only if $\bar{p}_{c,t}/p_{e,n,t} < \bar{p}_{c,t}/u_{e,n,t}$, which only occurs if the unit direct cost for the novel product below the average price of competing products and the value of $n_{e,n,t}$ is substantially less than one.

Keeping the price-cost ratio high during the origination phase generates profits to provide internal finance for investment in capacity expansion and can help in attracting external finance. Perhaps, even leading to acquisition by venture capitalists or an established firm with cash flow to invest in rapid expansion of production capacity. Pioneering customers provide a market for limited output in the origination phase, even when the price of the novel product doesn't provide much better value than alternatives.[8]

During the adoption phase of the meso trajectory of the novel product, a key consideration is the threat of entry from imitators. The benchmark for prices of

---

[8] The pricing strategy for the origination phase as presented here corresponds to the practice of price skimming discussed by Dean (1969), while pricing strategy for the adoption phase discussed

competing products shifts from the prices of established distant competitors to prices likely to be charged by imitators. Sylos-Labini (1962) suggests the entry-limiting price is equal to the unit cost of a small-scale potential entrant. Prices above this level attract at least some entry. A trade-off exists between ceding market share to imitators and generating internal finance for expansion of production capacity, as discussed in Section 3.3.3.

In the retention phase of the meso trajectory for the novel product, there are imitators operating in the industry. Here, price dynamics depend on the interaction between the innovating firm and its imitators, who have unit direct cost that may be below, equal, or above those of the innovator. Price determination for this situation is a special case of price theory for industries disrupted by innovation, which is presented in Chapter 5.

Learning and specialisation of labour in production occurring during the adoption and retention phases of the meso trajectory for novel products contribute to sharp decreases in the cost of production. The dynamics of differential firm growth as discussed in Chapter 5 ensure that cost decreases pass into price decreases, with stable or falling price-cost ratios. Thus, a sharp downward path for prices of novel products relative to those of established goods and services is commonly observed. Witness the experience of prices for computers, mobile phones, electric vehicles, and internet services over recent decades.

3.4 Summary

Firms are heterogeneous, even across firms producing similar products. They face an uncertain future and operate with limited knowledge. Their behaviour is generally regulated by rules and routines, particularly for large firms and mega-firms, who depend on such rules and routines to coordinate the activities of many individuals with specialised knowledge and skills. These rules and routines vary across firms, contributing to the variety of firm behaviour.

Several dimensions of differences among firms are examined in this chapter. First, differences in firm size, scope, and organisation are addressed, with emphasis on differences between small, large, and mega-firms. Second, the orientations of firms are distinguished in terms of survival, profit, growth, and innovation. Third, price-maker firms are distinguished from price-taker firms, both in terms of market conditions facing the firms and the behaviours they adopt in response. Fourth, price leadership is discussed as involving both price-taker behaviour (for the followers) and price-maker activity (for the leader).

---

next is related to what Dean labels as penetration pricing. For an updated discussion in the marketing literature of the analysis of price skimming and penetration pricing, see Chatterjee (2009).

Finally, the pricing analysis is applied to determining price for a novel product with pricing behaviour changing between the origination, adoption, and retention phases of the meso trajectory for the novel product.

Part II Meso

4 Market Order

Preliminary to the analysis of how prices are determined in an evolving economy, I consider the theoretical role of prices when an economy is experiencing development from within. In Schumpeter's ([1934] 1961, 1939) theory of economic development and the business cycle there are two roles for price information. Prices provide information to coordinate transactions and encourage efficient resource allocation, and they provide information to entrepreneurs and their financiers to use in assessing the profitability of potential innovations.

Schumpeter argues under normal economic conditions price information is reliable and transactions are well coordinated. Reliable price information is useful to entrepreneurs and their financiers in assessing the profitability of innovations, thereby supporting a wave of innovations. However, innovations disrupt normality, undermining the coordinating role of prices. Price information becomes less reliable, leading to a downswing in innovative activity that continues until the price system adjusts and more normal conditions return.[9]

4.1 Coordinating Price

Schumpeter (1939) refers to a theoretical norm for price in discussing the prices that occur when innovations are fully absorbed in the economy. Marshall, his followers, and Sraffians use related concepts of normal price and reproduction price, respectively, to refer to the prices that occur in the long period, when external disturbing influences have dissipated (Bloch 2022). Forces determining the long-period price in these approaches are conceptually distinct from each other (Bloch 2020).

For reasons explained in remaining chapters, especially Chapter 7, Schumpeter's concept of a theoretical norm for prices is rejected as being logically incoherent and unhelpful in evolutionary price theory. Instead, coordinating price is suggested as an appropriate theoretical concept for price. The coordinating price is a price consistent with orderly exchanges between buyers and sellers in a market in the short period, but subject to change over time as the

---

[9] The co-evolution of prices and innovative activity in a two-sector model is examined in Almudi et al (2021).

market develops from within. No concept of a disturbance-free or long-period price is offered for evolutionary price theory as disturbance is always present or emergent in the evolving economy. Evolutionary price theory is a theory of prices in motion.

The remainder of this chapter discusses the role of price information in coordinating buyer and seller activities in an evolving economy. The concept of market order replaces the concept of market equilibrium in mainstream price theory. First discussed is price determination in orderly markets with large numbers of buyers and sellers, adapting the concepts of supply and demand to an evolutionary context. Following is a discussion of using administered prices to create order in markets dominated by a small number of sellers or buyers. With either market-determined prices or administered prices, coordinating price is the theoretical price concept for market order.

Buyers and sellers follow fixed routines of behaviour of the types discussed in the last two chapters. Constancy is also assumed for the structure of production, skills, resources, and equipment, so the analysis is along the lines of Marshall's (1920) analysis of the short period. Analysis in the next chapter addresses the process of adjustment of routines and the structure of production over time, roughly corresponding to Marshall's concept of the long-period adjustment. The coordinating price follows a trajectory from one short period to the next during the adjustment process.

Throughout this chapter and the next, the analysis focusses on individual markets. The individual market is a sub-system of the economy. Order in a market is subject to disturbance from within if there is incomplete adjustment to impact of innovations, as is discussed in the next chapter. Order in a market is also subject to external disturbance as other markets adjust to the impact of innovations. The analysis of individual markets is extended to the interaction across markets, and to the aggregate economy, in Part III.

4.2 Spontaneous Market Order

The market economy is a system that connects groups of heterogeneous agents and organisations, individuals, households, firms, regulatory agencies, governments and others, who have disparate knowledge, skills, and resources. Agency implies objectives or goals and the means to achieve these goals. Connections involve the exchange of information between agents that result in the distributed and simultaneous attainment of goals. Prices are essential components of this information providing terms on which transactions occur in the pursuit of these goals.

For analytical purposes the market economy can be thought of as a collection of market sub-systems. In a complex economy as a system, interactions are numerous within sub-systems relative to interactions between sub-systems. Thus, a single system can be considered as if it were isolated or considered as connected to other systems to form a hierarchical or layered interaction (Arthur 2015).

Buyers and sellers, operating under their respective routines as discussed in Chapters 2 and 3, generally interact in markets under conditions of imperfect information. Each buyer is aware of a subset of information about the prices, characteristics, and availability of goods or services being offered by sellers, while sellers are generally imperfectly informed of the extent of interest from buyers. Not every buyer or every seller need end with the best possible deal or even with a transaction. Yet, there can still be spontaneous order among buyers and sellers in the market.

Nelson (2013) rejects assumptions of optimisation and equilibrium from mainstream analysis of markets as inconsistent with continuing endogenous structural change in an evolving economy. Nonetheless, most markets in an evolving economy are far from chaotic at any point in time. Nelson (2013, p. 29) suggests applying the concept of market order, providing the definition, 'An orderly market is characterized by a set of routines established over time that when employed by potential buyers and potential sellers are tuned to each other and generally result in transactions that are satisfactory for most parties on both sides of the market.' He then suggests using supply and demand analysis based on behavioural routines, rather than optimisation, to analyse price determination in orderly markets with large numbers of both buyers and sellers. Order is created as the routines of buyers lead to increased purchases at lower prices, while supplier routines result in offering to sell more at higher prices.[10]

An orderly market need not have a single price, even for a homogeneous product. Imperfect information about prices, even about the identity of potential buyers and sellers, means transactions can occur at differing prices. Likewise, there can be missed transactions when willing buyers and sellers aren't connecting. Neither price nor quantity need be fully determined by the willingness of buyers and sellers to engage in transactions.

With imperfect price information and imperfect connections between buyer and sellers, supply and demand are not interpretable as the single valued functions used in mainstream economics. Rather, they represent sets of buyers

---

[10] Nelson (2013, p. 26) attributes the concept of market order to Hayek (1948) and suggests this interpretation of market outcomes is 'much more in the spirit of Alfred Marshall's characterization of what lies behind prevailing prices and quantities purchased and sold in parts of the economy that are not changing rapidly, than the treatment in contemporary textbooks.'

and sellers willing to transact at various prices. In Figure 1, the demand set boundary, D, shows the maximum price (willingness to pay) that can be achieved for various volumes of a product offered to buyers, while the supply set boundary, S, shows the minimum price required to elicit various volumes of product from sellers. The intersection of the boundaries D and S gives a theoretical maximum quantity, Q_C^* if all possible transactions occur at the coordinating price, p_C^*.

If all potential buyers and sellers are connected and if all transactions occur at the price where the boundaries of the demand and supply sets intersect in Figure 1, p_C^*, we have the special case of perfect market order,

$$Q_c = \sum_i^n (q_i) = Q_C^* \text{ and } p_c = \sum_i^n (q_i p_i)/Q_c = p_C^*,$$
$$\text{as } p_i = p_C^* \text{ for all } i \text{ in } n, \tag{4.1}$$

where q_i and p_i are the quantity and price for the ith transaction out of n. Importantly, Equation (4.1) doesn't imply the market is in equilibrium. Equilibrium implies the absence of any possibility of change from within. Perfect market order occurs when all possible buyers and sellers are connected and all trades occur at the coordinating price, p_C^*. The possibility of endogenous change remains. Also, there is no implied tendency for perfect market order to be restored if trades occur away from the coordinating price.

The outcome of perfect market order is extremely unlikely in a competitive market with imperfect information and incomplete connections between buyers and sellers. Individual voluntary transactions can occur anywhere within the set boundaries in Figure 1. Not all possible transactions need occur, and many transactions will occur at prices above or below the coordinating price.

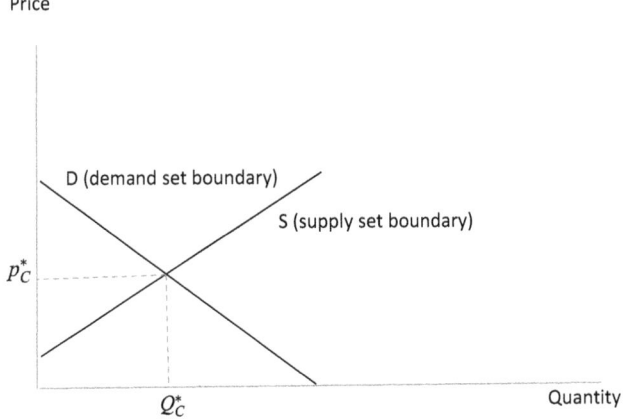

Figure 1 Order with a market-determined price

Nelson's (2013, p. 29) definition of market order doesn't require perfect order in terms of Equation (4.1); rather, he requires only, 'transactions that are satisfactory for most parties on both sides of the market.' In an orderly market Q_c won't fall too far short of Q_C^* and p_c won't diverge too far from p_C^*. Additionally, to avoid widespread buyer or seller regret, the variance of p_i should not be large. Thus, conditions for market order are of the form,

$$Q_c = Q_C^* - \alpha, p_c \approx p_C^*, \alpha < \varphi \text{ and } \text{Var}(p_i^*) = \sum_1^m (p_i - p_c^*)^2 / m < \theta, \quad (4.2)$$

where φ and θ are upper limits on missed voluntary transactions and variance of transaction prices, respectively. These requirements for a market to be considered orderly lack quantitative precision, at least at this stage of development of the theory of market order.

Institutional arrangements can be expected to affect the extent to which quantity traded in a market falls short of Q_C^*, the degree to which average price diverges from p_C^*, and the size of the variance of p_i. Many types of institutions exist, from local farmer's markets to organised commodity exchanges, such as the London Metals Exchange and the Chicago Board of Trade. Institutions have evolved over time from medieval town markets to internet platforms, such as eBay. Changes in transport, communications, and information technology have all had an impact. All of this is ignored in mainstream analysis through assuming perfect information and zero transaction costs.

Bid and ask prices on organised commodity exchanges provide information on the willingness to trade of buyers and sellers. However, such bid and ask prices can't be directly interpreted as indicating boundaries to the demand and supply sets for the commodity being traded. A buyer certainly won't bid more than their willingness to pay, but they may bid less hoping to secure supply at a lower price. Likewise for supplier offer prices. The variability of transaction prices over any trading period makes such strategies plausible if not always successful.

Data on transactions from organised commodity markets include the activities of traders who are neither suppliers nor users of the commodity, but who seek to profit from buying cheap and selling dear. If they are successful, the activities of these traders tend to stabilise prices, helping to achieve market order. Yet, there are occasions when price volatility on organised commodity markets exceeds bounds consistent with market order, even occasions when market rules on excessive price movements lead to trade being halted with buyers and sellers unable to complete any transactions. More generally, market order, even with the loose bounds of Equation (4.2), is not guaranteed by competition among large numbers of buyers and sellers.

Heterogeneity of buyers and sellers is fully compatible with market order. Indeed, variation in bids across buyers provides an explanation for the downward slope of the demand set boundary in Figure 1, as variation in offers across suppliers explains the upward slope of the supply set boundary. For example, market demand may consist of buyers who only purchase a single unit at varying maximum prices, while market supply may consist of sellers who offer a fixed number of units each at varying minimum prices that are above their average variable unit cost of production. Mainstream assumptions of declining marginal utility for each word buyer and increasing marginal cost for word seller are unnecessary.

Evolutionary change is also fully compatible with market order. Learning by buyers as discussed in Chapter 2 leads to changes in the demand set boundary in Figure 1, while growth and innovation by firms as discussed in Chapter 3 lead to changes in the supply set boundary. Whether these changes in set boundaries flow through into equal or proportionate changes in the quantities traded or the average price of the product depends on institutional structure, on information flow and connections between buyers and sellers in the market. Still, in an orderly market, changes in Q_C^* and p_C^* can be expected to flow through roughly in proportion to changes in the values of Q_c and p_c.[11]

Changes due to external shocks move the boundaries of the demand and supply sets in Figure 1, much as do the changes arising from evolution when consumers are learning, or when firms are growing and innovating. The analysis of market order presented here encompasses both evolutionary change from within and the impact of external shocks that are emphasised in mainstream analysis. Mainstream analysis of equilibrium is restricted to the impact of external shocks because evolutionary change from within is inconsistent with equilibrium.

Econometric practices for using series of market quantities and prices as observations of underlying theoretical values tend to treat observations of prices symmetrically with observations of quantities. This treatment is not correct for orderly markets, according to the analysis leading to the conditions in Equation (4.2). While the average value of price for all transactions in the market is an unbiased approximation of the coordinating price, p_C^*, the total quantity traded is a downward biased approximation of the quantity traded under perfect market

---

[11] Almudi et al (2021) present a coevolution bi-sectoral model with price co-determination to explain, through their dynamic analysis, how spontaneous market orders and multisector-prices are determined in evolving settings, in operational time with disequilibrium exchanges, and not in a Walrasian (or Neo-Walrasian) vacuum.

order, Q_C^*. Estimation methods, such as ordinary least squares, that assume a symmetric disturbance of disturbances around a theoretical value are valid for estimating relationships with price as a stochastic variable. However, when quantity is the stochastic variable, a method that takes account of the one-sided distribution of the disturbances, such as stochastic frontier analysis, is required.

Nelson (2013, p. 33) is certainly on the right track in suggesting, 'the basic arguments in price theory about how changes in demand and supply affect prevailing prices and quantities hold up under the theory of market order I have been developing, but without the encumbering baggage about the characteristics of market equilibrium.' He adds cautions about needing to interpret supply and demand curves as heuristic simplifications, about not all potential transactions occurring, and about the importance of institutional details. Each of these cautions is reflected in the discussion earlier.

Importantly, Nelson (2013, p. 38) points out that the tools of price theory based on market order are useful for short-run analysis, but 'Understanding of long run economic change requires a very different mode of analysis, which is what modern evolutionary economics is mostly about'. Adjustment of prices and quantities to major innovations is the subject of the next chapter. First, the following section discusses extending the notion of market order to markets without large numbers of sellers or buyers.

4.3 Administered Market Order

Bloch and Metcalfe (2018) extend application of the concept of market order to markets with dominant sellers or buyers. They note the use of administrative routines by dominant firms to set prices fits well with the presumptions of evolutionary analysis, providing a reasoned response to the need for internal control to achieve strategic objectives in a complex environment. Firms with radically new products use administered prices to establish market order, even though demand curves in the usual sense don't exist. Administered prices combine with routines to deal with unexpected fluctuations in demand or supply, such as maintaining inventories or underutilised productive capacity for sellers and accumulating superfluous inventories for buyers. These routines provide an alternative to price adjustments as a means of achieving market order.

As explained in Chapter 3, setting an administered price generally involves multiplying a measure of normal unit cost by a desired price-to-cost ratio exceeding one. With the unit cost measure based on operating at normal output, changes in output need not have immediate effect on prices. In contrast, changes in operating cost due to changes in input prices are fully and quickly passed on to changes in product price. Thus, the pattern of changes in administered prices in response to demand and cost changes is different from the pattern of changes in coordinating price in markets with spontaneous market order, where changes in both demand and cost are partially passed on to price changes.

Maintaining market order with administered prices represents strategic behaviour of firms. For example, with prices set by the seller, market order requires that buyers are generally able to obtain their desired quantities at those prices. Manufacturing firms are usually able to satisfy buyer demand at the set price by operating with substantial inventories or underutilised capacity to accommodate fluctuations in demand or potential supply chain disruptions. The quantities traded are satisfactory to the sellers in the sense that they are consistent with the strategy of survival and growth in the long period.

Quantity determination in an orderly market for a product j with an administered price is depicted in Figure 2. The demand set depicted is of similar form to that in Figure 1, while the supply set shows any quantity is available at the administered price, p_j, up to the capacity of the seller, q_j^x. If all potential buyers can identify the seller and the quantity buyers desire at p_j is below capacity, $q_j < q_j^x$, then all potential transactions are completed and occur at the administered price, which then constitutes a coordinating price. All buyers willing to pay the administered price are served and the quantity sold is consistent with the firm's strategy.

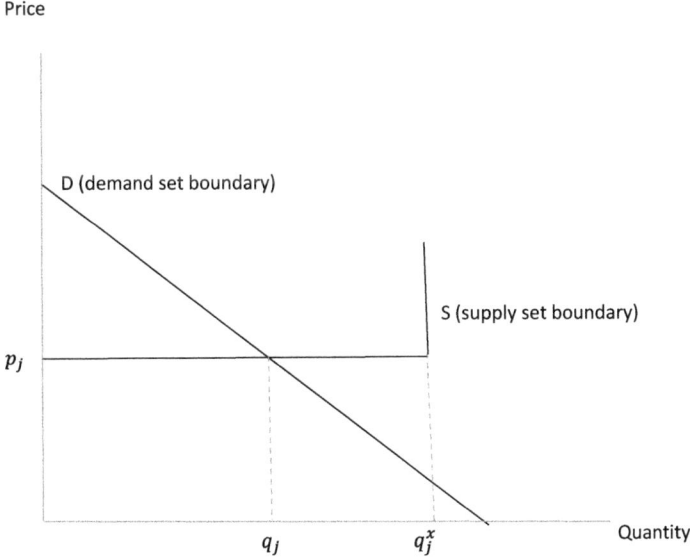

Figure 2 Order with an administered price

Multiple firms selling similar products are grouped into an industry for purposes of data collection and for analysing firm interactions, including differential firm growth. Industry quantity sold, Q_A, is given by adding up quantities of individual firms (in physical units) and average price, $\bar{p}_A$, is given by summing values sold across firms and dividing by total quantity sold,

$$Q_A = \sum_{j=1}^{n}(q_j) \text{ and } \bar{p}_A = \left[\sum_{j=1}^{n}(p_j * q_j)\right]/Q_A \tag{4.3}$$

When the same price is charged by all sellers, $p_j = \bar{p}_A$, and each seller is serving all potential customers at that price, then, $Q_A = Q_A^*$, where Q_A^* is the maximum quantity of sales with voluntary transactions. Perfect market order is achieved with the industry average price as a coordinating price, $\bar{p}_A = p_A^*$

Market order can be considered in a broader context when firms set differing administered prices. Each seller sets a price and buyers choose amongst the sellers based on the information they have available about sellers and their prices. Missed sales are possible if buyers aren't aware of sellers whose price is acceptable. Also, buyers need not find the best possible deal. Provided sellers have sufficient capacity to supply all prospective buyers, market order is achieved when,

$$Q_A = Q_A^* - \alpha \, , \bar{p}_A = p_A^* + \beta, \ \alpha < \varphi, \beta < \Phi,$$
$$\text{and } Var(p_j) = \sum_{j}^{m}(p_j - p_A^*)^2/m \leq \theta, \tag{4.4}$$

where φ, Φ and θ are upper limits on missed voluntary transactions, missed best buys, and variance of transaction prices, respectively, that might be regarded as consistent with market order.

Markets with administered prices are likely to be well ordered, at least in the absence of the type of disruptions discussed in Chapter 5. While each firm faces its own demand set and has its own administered price and supply capacity, the demand sets and determination of administered price are clearly related. As discussed in Chapter 3, price leadership is a common feature of theories of price determination for markets with administered markets. With price leadership and similar products due to competitive imitation, the variance of p_j is likely to be low and the market price and quantity are likely to closely approach their levels associated with perfect market order. Indeed, if all firms set their price equal to that of the market leader, there is no variance in price in the market and the leader's price is a coordinating price.

For the reasons discussed earlier, markets with administered prices are likely to be more orderly than those where prices are determined by the competitive interactions of large numbers of buyers and sellers.[12] Administered prices also are expected to react differently to external shocks than do competitive market prices. As explained in Chapter 3, demand shocks are unlikely to affect administered prices, at least in the short period, while competitive market prices are expected to rise and fall as product demand rises and falls. Thus, ratios in the form of $p_C/\bar{p}_A$ can be expected to be procyclical, rising (falling) with positive (negative) demand fluctuations. Further, changes in input prices are likely to flow through to the administered product price roughly in proportion to the input's share of variable cost, while input prices are expected to pass through only partially into product markets in competitive markets.

Empirically, the administered prices for manufactured goods are generally stable over time relative to the prices of primary commodities used as foodstuffs and raw materials that are largely determined in competitive commodity markets. Building on the work of Kalecki (1971), Bloch and Sapsford (2000) show the world average of primary commodity prices responds much more strongly to short-term changes in world industrial output than does the corresponding world average of manufactured goods prices. Bloch and Sapsford (2013) further show the long business cycle associated with Schumpeterian waves of innovation is characterised by procyclical movements in the ratio of primary commodity prices to the average price of manufactured goods.

4.4 Summary

Following on from Nelson (2013), market order is proposed as a replacement for market equilibrium as a concept for analysing price determination in evolutionary economics. Equilibrium implies no tendency to change from within, which is inconsistent with theory that treats evolution as an endogenous process. Order requires only that most buyers and sellers can execute trades within the bounds of their acceptable prices and desired quantities. Markets with large numbers of buyers and sellers can be orderly in the sense that both the quantity sold and average price approximate those associated with perfect market order, even though individual transaction prices may deviate from that level. The price associated with perfect market order, which is designated the

---

[12] Market equilibrium occurs with conditions equivalent to the conditions for perfect market order, namely all transactions occur at a single price and all potential transactions are completed. These conditions are unlikely to be met, especially in competitive markets. Thus, comparing efficiency of allocation between competitive and imperfectly competitive markets based on equilibrium positions is inherently flawed. Accounting for the differential degree of order with competitive versus administered prices is required. Of course, the static criterion of market efficiency is generally of much less concern to evolutionary economists than the dynamic criteria of growth and development.

coordinating price, serves as an analytical reference point for evolutionary price theory in parallel to the short-period equilibrium price of mainstream theory.

When prices are set administratively by dominant sellers (buyers), most buyers (sellers) generally are able to obtain their desired quantity of purchases (sales) at the set price. The maintenance of excess capacity or inventories by the sellers or buyers increases the proportion of possible transactions that complete. Price leadership is common in markets with administered prices, which tends to reduce the variation in price across transactions. In the extreme case, there is only one price at which all transactions take place, making this price a coordinating price if there is sufficient capacity for all buyers willing to pay this price. Thus, markets with administered prices tend to be orderly, at least in the short period.

Market order with either competitive or administered prices is supported by stable behavioural routines for both buyers and sellers. Disruptive innovations, such as new products, new production processes, or new market infrastructure, challenge the ability of buyers and sellers to change their routines. Consumers change their budget allocation, firms change their products, production methods and sources of input supply; robots displace workers, web platforms displace brick and mortar outlets, electric engines displace internal combustion engines, etcetera. Disruption of markets and the ensuing process of price adjustment are discussed in the next chapter. System-wide disruption and structural changes at the meso and macro level are then discussed in Part III.

5 Disrupted Markets and Differential Firm Growth

Variations in the quantity of bids or offers due to external influences change the coordinating price, much as shifts in supply and demand change the equilibrium price in mainstream price theory. However, the coordinating price also changes due to endogenous processes. One such process is creative destruction following innovations, with heterogeneity in firm characteristics leading to differential firm growth.

In this chapter, two approaches are used to analyse differential firm growth. One approach, with market-determined prices, closely follows Nelson and Winter (1982) by assuming price is determined to clear the market. Another approach, with administered prices, follows Metcalfe (1998) and assumes price is set using pricing routines of the type discussed in Chapter 3. In both variants, higher profitability of successful innovators drives the expansion of their production capacity relative to non-innovating rivals.

Before examining the price dynamics from creative destruction, the precursor role of price information in the introduction of variety through innovations is examined in Section 5.1. Schumpeter argues reliable price information enables entrepreneurs to determine the profitability of their potential innovations and to obtain bank finance for acquiring means of production. While banks no longer feature as prominently in the financing of innovations, reliable price information still contributes to success in seeking external financing for innovation.

Once innovators have overcome the barrier to external financing and successfully established themselves, they can build on their success by reinvesting profit in expansion of their production capacity. This process of internal accumulation is at the core of the two approaches to price dynamics through differential firm growth discussed in Section 5.2. Internal accumulation also features prominently in Steindl's (1976]) analysis of dynamic competition in capitalism, which is discussed in Section 5.3 along with other post-Keynesian approaches to price determination.

5.1 Reliable Price Information and Financing of Innovations

Market order is under constant threat. Some forms of incremental change, such as gradual growth in demand, are compatible with the maintenance of market order. However, with disruptive innovations, the rules and routines that regulate the behaviour of buyers and sellers no longer lead to expected results. The introduction of substantial novelty into the economy leads to behavioural changes and structural transformation.

Evolving systems are systems open to novelty stimulated unpredictably by their internal operation. Price information is used for market calculation necessary to achieve order. However, as Loasby (1999, 2003) insists, creativity and imagination are equally important as calculative ability in understanding how an economy works. Making and breaking of connections is then reflected in the changing economic structure, which generates further flows of innovation. Prices are essential to this process, through stimulating investment in innovation and then financing investment in expansion of productive capability to diffuse the innovation.

Mainstream economics recognises the coordination aspect of price information in markets, but not the role of price information in stimulating innovations or the impact of innovations on the reliability of price information. While prices underpin the prevailing order, their correlating function, they also guide the formation of conjectures that challenge the prevailing order by setting yardsticks any challenger must meet to displace some existing activity. This is the de-correlating function of prices, to give rise to conjectures about new possibilities and the emergence of novelty. In establishing market order, the price system generates the impetus to challenge that order.

The exchange of information is also a principal reason for continuous and unpredictable changes in the levels of understanding held by agents. Not all new knowledge is reliable (Ziman 1978). A means to test the validity of new conjectures is essential. As Potts (2001, p. 418) notes regarding the dual role of markets, 'They are spaces where existing knowledge is coordinated and where new knowledge is tested.' Profitability is a price system test of innovations. Successful innovators use high profits to expand relative to their established rivals in the process of creative destruction.

Static analysis is not appropriate for evolutionary analysis according to Schumpeter ([1934] 1961, p. 64), who notes, 'Development in our sense is a distinct phenomenon, entirely foreign to what may be observed in the circular flow or in the tendency towards equilibrium.' Yet, the structure of prices at a point in time can still be usefully related to the movement of prices over time. The concepts of coordinating price and market order discussed in the last chapter are concepts related to analysis of the structure of prices at a point in time. In this chapter, the focus is on the movement of prices over time as part of the endogenous process of innovation-driven change under capitalism. In evolutionary price theory, the structure of prices and the movement through time are connected through creative destruction as is explained in Section 5.2.

Schumpeter's (1947) distinction between adaptive and creative responses is useful in an evolutionary understanding of the way creative agents, with their disparate imaginings of the future, react to the structure of prices. Responding to the existing price structure using established rules, routines, or habits is an adaptive response, which tends to maintain order. A creative response devises a new form of behaviour that is advantageous to the innovator, which tends to destroy order. To paraphrase a favourite Schumpeter example, responding to an increased volume of freight between cities in the early nineteenth century by increasing the number of mail coaches is an adaptive response, whereas building a railway is a creative response.[13]

5.1.1 Forecasting the Profitability of Innovations

The existing structure of prices, the price system in Schumpeter's (1939) terminology, provides a basis for calculating the profits obtainable from a potential innovation. Yet, future prices rather than current prices determine the realised profitability from investments in innovation. While some future prices can be secured using contracts, such opportunities are limited and non-existent for novel

---

[13] Illustrating what he means by the type of change he has in mind for development as a discontinuous process, Schumpeter ([1934] 1961, p. 64, n. 1) notes, 'Add successively as many mail coaches as you please, you will never get a railway.'

products. What determines the degree to which current prices can be taken as indicators of future prices?

Schumpeter (1939) points to innovation as the driver of changes to the price system. Without innovative activity, the economy can move smoothly through time. In the extreme case of the circular flow of an economy in a stationary state or with balanced growth, there is no need for structural change in the economy and no need for change to the price system. With innovations, structural adjustments are required, and changes to the price system provide information to buyers and sellers that facilitate these adjustments.

Schumpeter argues smooth movement of the economy through time is impossible under capitalism. With smooth movement, entrepreneurs rely on the unchanging price system in calculating the profitability of intended innovations. Innovations flourish, ending the smooth movement and unchanged price system.

Instead of smooth movement, Schumpeter argues innovations ebb and flow as the price system is disturbed and then adjusts. Reliable price information leads to a wave of innovations, a wave of innovations disturbs the price system, change in the price system depresses innovative activity, low innovative activity reduces disturbance of the price system. The sequence repeats indefinitely, providing capitalism with an unlimited, but uneven, driver of development. Schumpeter (1939) applies this approach to explaining the historical development of capitalism as a series of long waves or Kondratieff cycles lasting over a half-century each, starting with the Industrial Revolution.

5.1.2 Financing for Innovations

Schumpeter ([1934] 1961 and 1939) argues reliable price information and the ability to forecast the profitability of innovations encourages the introduction of innovations. Innovators need to acquire means of production without generally having ready access to finance. Schumpeter's archetypical innovator is an entrepreneurial outsider with limited personal wealth who seeks credit from banks. Reliable price information enhances the prospects of successfully obtaining a loan.

Later, Schumpeter ([1950] 1976) acknowledges the increasing role of large industrial firms in the introduction of innovations. Existing flows of profit allow these firms to internally finance innovations. Executive management allocates resources to an innovation based on calculations of prospective profitability, and chances of a project being approved increase with the reliability of the price information on which the calculations are based. Nowadays, venture capital is an important source of external finance for innovations by start-up firms, but reliable price information still contributes to the prospects of securing finance.

5.2 Differential Firm Growth and the Diffusion of Innovations

Once an innovation is in operation, realised profitability displaces prospective profitability as the criterion used by providers of external financing. The market test of profitability confirms or refutes the projections of entrepreneurs. More directly and importantly, realised profits provide internal financing for expansion by innovating firms. Successful innovators use their extra profits to expand relative to non-innovators. Price dynamics associated with differential firm growth constitute an essential element of evolutionary price theory and this section is devoted to presenting this theory.

Differential firm growth is identified as the mechanism for the diffusion of innovations in modern evolutionary economic analyses following Nelson and Winter (1982) and Metcalfe (1998). Output from innovating firms grows relative to that from their established rivals. Contra to the instantaneous and costless diffusion of innovations assumed in mainstream economics, diffusion takes time and involves creative destruction. Creative destruction means the decline and eventual extinction of many established firms, along with obsolescence for capital equipment and redundancy for labour skills.

Metcalfe (1998) analyses industry evolution in terms of changes in firm market shares. His approach is adapted here to examine the dynamics of the market share of a successful innovating firm, denoted by the subscript e. Here, the innovating firm is a new entrant, is externally funded, and is small. The firm then grows faster than the industry average,

$$s_{e,i,t} = s_{e,i,0}\left[\left(1+g_{e,i,t}\right)/\left(1+g_{i,t}\right)\right]^t, \text{ where } \left[\left(1+g_{e,i,t}\right)/\left(1+g_{i,t}\right)\right] > 1 \quad (5.1)$$

where $s_{e,i,t}$ is the share of the innovating firm in industry sales, $g_{e,i,t}$ is the innovating firm's rate of growth of sales and $g_{i,t}$ is the rate of growth of industry sales. Taking the partial derivative of (5.1) with respect to time gives the rate of change of the share of the entrepreneurial firm,

$$\partial s_{e,i,t}/\partial t = s_{e,i,t} * ln\left[\left(1+g_{e,i,t}\right)/\left(1+g_{i,t}\right)\right] \approx s_{e,i,t} * \left(g_{e,i,t} - g_{i,t}\right) > 0 \quad (5.2)$$

Growth in the market share of the innovating firm comes at the expense of non-innovating firms, denoted by the subscript m, with the collective share of non-innovating firms given by,[14]

---

[14] Focusing attention of the group of existing firms excludes consideration of entry and exit of firms.

$$s_{m,i,t} = \sum\nolimits_{k=1}^{n} s_{k,i,t} = 1 - s_{e,i,t} \qquad (5.3)$$

When growth in the innovating firm's sales exceeds industry growth, the rate of growth of sales for remaining firms as a group is below the rate of industry growth,

$$s_{m,i,t} * g_{m,i,t} = g_{i,t} - s_{e,i,t} * g_{e,i,t} \qquad (5.4)$$

The extent of this shortfall increases with the innovating firm's share of sales, becoming negative as the share of the innovating grows,

$$g_{m,i,t} = g_{i,t} - [s_{e,i,t}/(1 - s_{e,i,t})](g_{e,i,t} - g_{i,t}) \qquad (5.5)$$

Continued growth of the innovating firm requires expansion of production capacity and increased uptake from buyers. Both are linked to pricing but in opposite directions. High prices and profits provide internal financing for expansion as discussed in Section 5.1.2, while low prices stimulate sales to buyers.

The tension between the two informational roles of prices is analysed as a process of differential firm growth. Section 5.2.1 analyses the process in markets consisting of price-taker firms producing a homogenous product with price determined in the market by equating full-capacity production and demand. Section 5.2.2 analyses the process in markets with imperfect competition and administered prices. Section 5.3 then provides a comparison to post-Keynesian theories of pricing, particularly the work of Steindl (1976).

5.2.1 Market-Determined Prices

Nelson and Winter (1982) examine Schumpeterian competition among initially identical firms seeking improved production techniques through R&D expenditure. Each firm has a routine deciding how much, if anything, to spend on R&D, which gives them of a probability of finding a cost-reducing innovation. Successful R&D allows the firm to increase output per unit of input and reduce the cost of each unit produced. Linear production technology is assumed, so that unit operating cost is constant up to capacity and then rises vertically. Firms expand capacity over time based on realised profitability.

The analysis of the impact a cost-reducing innovation is illustrated in Figure 3. All firms start with an operating cost of u per unit and a full cost of c per unit. Combined production capacity is Q_c, which leads to a coordinating price of p_c determined by the interaction of buyers and sellers. If the gap between price and unit cost just covers depreciation and R&D expenditures,

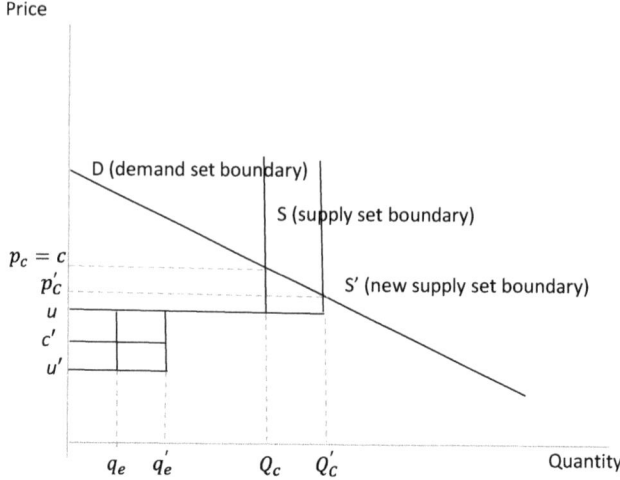

Figure 3 Competitive price with cost-reducing innovation

price equals full cost per unit of output for all producers. No net investment occurs and coordinating price and quantity remain at p_c and Q_c, respectively.

The initial impacts of cost-reducing innovation on costs, productive capacity, and price are that a successful innovation reduces the unit operating cost of the innovating firm to u' and the unit full cost to c' for q_e units of output. Nelson and Winter assume innovations increase output without any change in inputs, which implicitly treats the innovation as increasing productive capacity. Instead, it is assumed here that operating cost per unit of output falls but there is initially no change in productive capacity at the innovating firm, which provides a clearer separation of the impact of cost reduction from that of capacity expansion.

Industry output is initially unaffected by the innovation, so there is initially no change in price following the cost-reducing innovation. The innovating firm is earning extra profits at the prevailing price and, in response, invests in additional productive capacity. Output at other firms is unaffected. If capacity at the innovating firm expands from q_e to q'_e, industry output expands to Q'_C and the coordinating price falls to p'_C.

Even after the fall in price, price remains above unit full cost for the innovating firm, so that firm continues to earn net profit and continues to expand its production capacity. Its extra output contributes to further declines in price. The reduced price is below the unit full cost for non-innovating firms, which means their net profits are negative. They continue operating as long as price remains above unit operating cost, but cease investments in capacity expansion. Thus, the market share of the innovating firm expands along with growth in the market.

In the Nelson and Winter model, each firm maintains the same R&D routine over time, with at least some non-innovating firms spending on innovative or imitative R&D. There is also continued spending on innovative R&D from the innovating firm. In each period, there is a positive probability that such spending results in a successful innovation. These innovations reduce the unit cost of one or more non-innovating firms to c' in the case of imitative R&D, or possibly to some level below c' in the case of innovative R&D. Continued R&D spending by the innovating firm can also result in lowering unit cost below c'.

Nelson and Winter analyse a full cycle of evolutionary process, including generating variety in technology through cost-reducing innovation, reproducing the technology through investment in expanding production capacity, and selection of technology through differential firm growth. Variation in technology is the outcome of a stochastic process, so their analysis relies on computer simulation models to analyse the dynamics of innovations, costs, profits, investments, and market shares.

Metcalfe (2007) narrows the focus of analysis to the reproduction and selection impacts of differential firm growth that are amenable to analytical solutions. The products of all firms are homogenous and are sold at a single price. Unit cost differences in this environment translate inversely proportionally to price-cost ratios,

$$(\pi_{k,i,t}/\pi_{j,i,t}) = 1/(c_{k,i,t}/\ c_{j,i,t}) \tag{5.6}$$

Adapting assumptions from the Nelson and Winter (1982) model to the limited scope of Metcalfe's (2007) analysis, the rate of growth of productive capacity at the kth firm, $g_{k,i,t}$, equals its net investment divided by capital in the prior period. Thus, $g_{k,i,t}$ equals the amount by which the firm's ratio of price to unit full cost, $\pi_{k,i,t-1}$, exceeds one multiplied by its ratio of net investment to net profit, $\theta_{k,i,t-1}$, and divided by its ratio of capital stock to full cost, $\Phi_{k,i,t-1}$,

$$g_{k,i,t} = (\pi_{k,i,t-1} - 1)(\theta_{k,i,t-1}/\Phi_{k,i,t-1}) \tag{5.7}$$

Metcalfe (1998) suggests an analogy between differential firm growth dynamics and replicator dynamics in biology. Fitness in biology is associated with a sub-species increasing its share of the population to which the sub-species belongs. Likewise, fitness of a firm is indicated by an increase in its share of sales among the population of firms selling similar products. An industry consisting of all such firms is a population with a common market selection environment. Metcalfe's measure of firm fitness is given by the rate of change in its market share, taken to be,

$$\partial s_{k,i,t}/\partial t = s_{k,i,t} * (g_{k,i,t} - g_{i,t}), \text{ where } \sum_{k=1}^{n}(\partial s_{k,i,t}/\partial t) = 0 \tag{5.8}$$

A positive value for the change in share in (5.8) indicates fitness. The innovating firm whose share growth equation is given in (5.2) exhibits fitness in this sense. Notably, fitness is a relative measure, indicated by the zero value for the sum of the fitness measure across the industry.[15]

To focus directly on the cost impact of the process of differential firm growth, unit cost at each firm is assumed to remain constant during this process and each firm is assumed to operate at full capacity. Industry average unit cost falls as the market share of the lowest cost firms grows. Taking the derivative of industry average unit cost with respect to time yields,

$$(d\bar{c}_{i,t}/dt) = \sum_{k=1}^{n}\left[s_{k,i,t} * (\partial c_{k,i,t}/\partial t) + c_{k,i,t} * (\partial s_{k,i,t}/\partial t)\right] \tag{5.9}$$

With no change in unit cost at any firm, the first term in brackets on the right-hand-side of (5.9) is zero. Imposing this condition and substituting for the change in market share from (5.8) yields,

$$(d\bar{c}_{i,t}/dt) = \sum_{k=1}^{n} s_{k,i,t} * \left[c_{k,i,t} * (g_{k,i,t} - g_{i,t})\right] < 0 \tag{5.10}$$

The right-hand-side of (5.10) gives the covariance of unit cost and growth rate across firms, which is negative when differential firm growth is driven by cost-reducing innovation. Metcalfe (1998) demonstrates that the covariance of unit cost and growth rate across firms declines with differential firm growth as market share concentrates in the low-cost firms.

The growth rate of industry supply is given by the weighted sum of growth rates over all firms in the industry, assuming all firms continue to operate and there is no entry. Substituting from the expression for firm growth rates from (5.7), and assuming for simplicity that all firms have the same internal accumulation rate, $\theta_{i,t}$, and the same capital-to-sales ratio, $\Phi_{i,t}$, yields,

$$g_{i,t}^{S} = \sum_{k=1}^{n} s_{k,i,t} * g_{k,i,t} = \sum_{k=1}^{n}\left[s_{k,i,t} *(\theta_{i,t}/\Phi_{i,t})(\pi_{k,i,t-1} - 1)\right]$$
$$= (\theta_{i,t}/\Phi_{i,t})(\bar{\pi}_{i,t-1} - 1) \tag{5.11}$$

Thus, the growth rate for industry supply is proportional to the margin by which the share-weighted average price-cost ratio for the industry, $\bar{\pi}_{i,t}$, exceeds one.

---

[15] Metcalfe (1998, p. 57) states, 'Fitness, we have claimed, is not an intrinsic property of firms but rather the consequence of the market co-ordination of rival behaviours: fitness results from the interaction between individual and environment and it is not an intrinsic feature of either.'

Balanced growth in supply and demand is achieved when the growth of supply equals the growth of demand. Decomposing demand growth into underlying growth at a constant price, given by $\alpha_{i,t}$, and the growth of demand due to price change yields,

$$g_{i,t}^D = \alpha_{i,t} + \eta_{i,t}(dp_{i,t}/dt)(1/p_{i,t}), \eta_{i,t} < 0 \qquad (5.12)$$

where $\eta_{i,t}$ is the price elasticity of industry demand. Equating (5.11) and (5.12) yields the price-cost ratio required for balanced growth of industry-level supply and demand,

$$\bar{\pi}_{i,t-1} = 1 + \left[\alpha_{i,t} + \eta_{i,t}(dp_{i,t}/dt)(1/p_{i,t})\right](\Phi_{i,t}/\theta_{i,t}) \qquad (5.13)$$

Balancing growth of supply and supply imposes perfect market order on an industry experiencing structural transformation through differential firm growth, which is implausible. The result is a thought experiment demonstrating implications for the industry of firm behavioural routines regarding investments in expanding productive capacity. Each firm implicitly assumes realised profitability is indicative of the profitability of this investment. As is shown next, they are correct as concerns their profitability relative to other firms in the industry, but the profitability of all firms falls over time. Past profitability is an imperfect guide to future profitability.[16] Analysis of the implications of differential firm growth without imposing perfect market order is flagged in Chapter 8 as a topic for further research.

Declining average unit cost in (5.10) increases the weighted average price-cost ratio for the industry unless offset by a decline in industry price. Initially, a higher price-cost ratio is required in (5.13) to finance the higher growth in demand with a declining industry price. However, the variance of unit cost across firms declines over time and approaches zero as the market share of low-cost firms approaches one. The rate of cost change in (5.10) converges on zero along with the rate of price change, implying a decline in the rate of growth in demand in (5.12) and in the price-cost ratio required for balancing in (5.13). The fall in the price-cost ratio means price falls faster than the rate of decline in weighted average unit cost.

For each firm, falling price implies a falling price-cost ratio as unit cost is assumed constant at the firm level. The growth rate for each firm declines according to (5.7). Balanced growth of industry supply and demand growth is

---

[16] Taking past profitability as a guide to investment behaviour contrasts to mainstream analysis that presumes firms correctly predict future profitability. The two approaches are alternative examples of simplifications for characterising investment behaviour in a world where the future is uncertain.

maintained through the rising share of low-cost firms with relatively high price-cost ratios and growth rates.

Declining industry price with constant unit cost for individual firms means the price-cost ratios for high-cost firms eventually drop below 1, which implies their net investment and growth is negative in (5.7). In the short period, depreciation sets a limit on how much negative net investment can occur in a period. The relationship between the price-cost ratio and firm growth in (5.7) no longer applies, but the course of industry dynamics slows only imperceptibly as the high-cost firms are already relatively small. If the price drops below unit operating cost for these firms, they cease production altogether, effectively exiting the industry, which speeds up market-share dynamics. Obsolescence is the cost of Schumpeterian competition for these firms, their fixed capital, and the specialised skills of their workers. Exit of firms is discussed in more detail in Chapter 6.

Assuming a smooth rate of growth in supply and demand is convenient for analytical purposes but not consistent with capitalist reality. As Schumpeter (1939) argues, innovation-driven growth under capitalism is inherently uneven. Growth of industry demand at constant price is decomposable into a trend component and an annual disturbance,

$$\alpha_{i,t} = \alpha_i + \varepsilon_{i,t}, \tag{5.14}$$

where α_i is a trend rate of growth and $\varepsilon_{i,t}$ is a disturbance term with zero mean and positive variance. How does this affect the dynamics of the market-determined price?

Fluctuations in the value of $\varepsilon_{i,t}$ in (5.14) create an imbalance between the growth in supply determined by the prior year's price-cost ratio and the current growth in demand. Price adjusts to balance the predetermined supply growth with the current demand growth. The current weighted average price-cost ratio then moves in the direction of price. If growth in supply follows the path indicated by (5.11), there is lagged adjustment to the temporary change in demand growth.

Lagged adjustment between demand and supply has long been studied in mainstream economics under the rubric of the cobweb model (Kaldor 1934, Ezekiel 1938). Oscillations in price are a feature of this analysis, with the oscillations being damped (explosive) when supply is less (more) responsive to price than is demand. Applying these conditions to equations (5.11) and (5.12) means damped oscillations occur if $\bar{\pi}_{i,t-1}(\theta_{i,t}/\Phi_{i,t}) < -\eta_{i,t}$, while explosive oscillations occur if the inequality sign is reversed.

5.2.2 Administered Prices

The analysis of differential firm growth in Metcalfe (1998) focuses on industries with differentiated products and imperfect competition. Prices are determined administratively by a normal pricing routine, where price is set to generate sufficient profit for financing expansion of capacity, taking account of the impact that price has on the growth rate of demand for the firm's product. The firm offers its full capacity output at that price.

Metcalfe has the growth rate for the firm's production capacity determined by the same relationship as in (5.7) but expressed with different notation. The kth firm's capacity growth rate equals its normal unit profit margin, given by the price-cost ratio minus one, multiplied by what Metcalfe calls the propensity to accumulate, $f_{k,i,t}$,

$$g^S_{k,i,t} = f_{k,i,t} * (\pi_{k,i,t} - 1), \; f_{k,i,t} > 0, \tag{5.15}$$

Comparing (5.15) to (5.7), $f_{k,i,t} = \theta_{k,i,t}/\Phi_{k,i,t}$, so the firm's propensity to accumulate equals its ratio of net investment to net profit divided by its capital-to-output ratio.[17]

Following an idea presented in Phelps and Winter (1970), Metcalfe presents a customer selection model in which the growth in demand for a firm's product is a linear function of the growth in industry demand and the difference between the firm's price and the weighted average industry price,

$$g^D_{k,i,t} = \alpha_{i,t} + \beta_{i,t}\left[\bar{p}_{i,t} - p_{k,i,t}\right], \text{ where } \beta_{i,t} > 0 \text{ and } \bar{p}_{i,t} = \sum_{k=1}^{n}\left(s_{k,i,t} * p_{k,i,t}\right) \tag{5.16}$$

The firm's normal pricing routine is to set an administered price that equates the growth in demand in (5.16) to the expansion of production capacity in (5.15), which is,

$$p_{k,i,t} = c_{k,i,t} * (\alpha_{i,t} + \beta_{i,t}\bar{p}_{i,t} + f_{k,i,t})/(f_{k,i,t} + \beta_{i,t}) \tag{5.17}$$

Thus, the firm's normal price increases with the growth rate for industry demand, $\alpha_{i,t}$, the weighted average price across the industry, $\bar{p}_{i,t}$, and the firm's unit cost, $c_{k,i,t}$.

Administered prices determined by (5.17) vary across firms along with variations in unit cost and propensity to accumulate. Simplifying by assuming

---

[17] Growth in capacity in (5.15) depends on the current price-cost ratio rather than the lagged price-cost ratio in (5.7) or (5.11). Firms setting administered prices base their prices on expected demand and unit cost rather than the realised values of price and unit cost that determine capacity expansion with market-determined prices. Therefore, fluctuations in demand, as in (5.14), don't affect the administered price or the amount of capacity expansion.

all firms have the same propensity to accumulate, $f_{i,t}$, and aggregating across all the firms in an industry,

$$\bar{p}_{i,t} = \left(1 + \alpha_{i;t}/f_{i;t}\right) * \bar{c}_{i,t} \qquad (5.18)$$

Taking total derivatives of both sides of (5.18), and assuming no change in $\alpha_{i,t}$ or $f_{i,t}$, implies the rate of change in the share-weighted average price equals the corresponding change in unit cost,

$$\left(d\bar{p}_{i,t}/dt\right)\left(1/\bar{p}_{i,t}\right) = \left(d\bar{c}_{i,t}/dt\right)\left(1/\bar{c}_{i,t}\right) \qquad (5.19)$$

Industry demand growth in (5.16) doesn't depend on the rate of change in product price at the industry level simplifies the analysis of dynamics of prices, costs, and market shares through differential firm growth.[18] It also suggests an analogy with the replicator dynamics of evolutionary biology. Metcalfe (1998, p. 61) refers to Fisher's Principle, the Fundamental Theorem of Natural Selection of R.A. Fisher (1930), which 'states that selection improves average fitness in the population, and that the rate of improvement is equal to the variance of fitness'.

The measure of fitness in Metcalfe's application of replicator dynamics is the relative growth of the firm. Application of Fisher's Principle implies that the simple average growth rate of firms across an industry falls as the variance of firm growth rates declines. However, the growth rate for industry supply remains equal to the growth of industry demand, with the rising market share of low-cost firms maintaining a constant weighted average growth rate for industry productive capacity.

Of more direct relevance to analysing price dynamics is the Secondary Theorem of Natural Selection, which Metcalfe (1998, p. 63) states, 'Consider any behavioural trait, then the rate of change population average of this trait and fitness across the population equals the covariance between that trait and fitness across the population'. Equation (5.10) provides an illustration of this theorem, with the rate of change of industry average unit cost equal to the covariance between firm unit cost and firm fitness (measured by the difference between its growth rate and the industry average).

Equation (5.10) is a generic expression that applies to any analysis of differential firm growth. Substituting from (5.16) through (5.18) into (5.15) uses the growth and pricing assumptions of the administered pricing analysis to

---

[18] Changes in industry average price have no impact on the aggregate demand across firm in (5.16), which differs from the inverse relationship between market demand and price in Section 5.2.1. Consequences for the dynamics of prices and price-cost ratios are discussed in Section 5.2.3.

Evolutionary Price Theory

derive an expression for firm growth in terms of the difference between its unit cost and the industry weighted average as follows,

$$g^S_{k,i,t} = a_{i,t} + [\bar{c}_{i,t} - c_{k,i,t}][(\beta_{i,t}*f_{i,t})/(f_{i,t}+\beta_{i,t})] \quad (5.20)$$

Further substituting from (5.20) into the generic expression in (5.10) for the rate of change in industry average unit cost yields,

$$(d\bar{c}_{i,t}/dt) = \sum_{k=1}^{n}[s_{k,i,t}*c_{k,i,t}*(c_{k,i,t}-c_{i,t})][(\beta_{i,t}*f_{i,t})/(f_{i,t}+\beta_{i,t})] < 0 \quad (5.21)$$

The first term in brackets in (5.21) is the weighted variance of unit cost across the industry. Thus, the variance of unit cost across firms is driving the differential firm growth process, which results in rising average efficiency as well as declining weighted average unit cost and price.

Metcalfe (1998, p. 51) shows the share-weighted variance of price across firms in the industry is proportional to the share-weighted variance in unit cost across the firms,

$$Var_s(p_{k,i,t}) = \sum_{k=1}^{n}[s_{k,i,t}*(p_{k,i,t}-\bar{p}_{i,t})^2] = Var_s(c_{k,i,t})*[f_{i,t}/(f_{i,t}+\beta_{i,t})]^2 \quad (5.22)$$

As the selection mechanism of differential firm growth reduces the variance of unit cost, the share-weighted variance of prices falls in tandem. Thus, the process of differential firm growth is degenerative with administered prices, as is the case for market-determined prices in Section 5.2.1. Heterogeneity is devoured by the process that drives differential growth.

5.2.3 Creative Destruction as a Competitive Process

Differential firm growth driven by profitability differences across firms leads to creative destruction. The share of industry output coming from low-cost firms increases, thereby reducing the weighted average unit cost for the industry, even though there is no change in unit cost at any firm. Both in the analysis of differentiated products with administered prices in Section 5.2.2 and in the analysis of homogenous products with market-determined prices in Section 5.2.1, this leads to declining prices for all firms.

Creative destruction is a form of competition within the industry, which only indirectly affects industry profitability.[19] As the price-cost ratio for each firm falls, the weighted average price-cost ratio for the industry changes only if the

---

[19] Metcalfe (1998, pp. 51–55) discusses how the concept of market power relates to his analysis of creative destruction through differential firm growth.

rate of growth of industry demand is impacted by declining prices. In the analysis with administered prices, industry demand is independent of price, so there is no growth in demand or change in industry profitability from declining product prices. In contrast, in the analysis of market-determined prices, a declining price boosts the growth of industry demand. Initially, this requires a higher price-cost ratio for balancing growth in supply with the growth of demand. However, as prices decline more slowly over time, the growth of demand also slows, so the price-cost ratio required for balancing growth in supply and demand declines.

Key to the analysis of pricing from creative destruction is the link between realised profitability for the firm and its investment in expanding production capacity, which leads to the differential firm growth. Without further innovation, the industry moves from disruption towards order through the disappearing share of high-cost firms in the market. Creative destruction is a process of self-ordering through self-transformation.

The desire to grow through reinvestment of profits is an essential premise for evolutionary price theory. Discussion in Chapter 3 suggests firms differ in their orientations, including the desire to grow. Metcalfe (1998) examines the implications for the process of creative destruction when there is heterogeneity in the propensity to accumulate across firms. The rate of decline in industry weighted average of unit cost and price is shown to depend on the covariance of over firms of unit cost and propensity to accumulate as well as on the variance over firms of unit cost. A firm with relatively low unit cost but a zero propensity to accumulate doesn't grow, which means its market share is continuously falling in a growing market.

Metcalfe notes access to external finance is generally easier for firms with higher profitability, which contributes to a negative covariance across firms between unit cost and the propensity to accumulate. This increases the rate of decline in weighted average unit cost and price for the industry. A capital market that encourages the growth of profitable enterprises thereby speeds the process of creative destruction. The interaction between internal and external financing of investment and the implications for price determination are further considered in connection with post-Keynesian price theory in the next section.

5.3 Post-Keynesian Parallels

Overlap between the administered pricing analysis of the previous section and the work of Kalecki (1971) is readily apparent in comparing the normal pricing routine in (5.17) to the Kaleckian pricing routine in (3.3). A key difference is the growth of industry demand is included in price determination in (5.17), whereas Kalecki treats the pricing coefficients m and n as determined by a range of factors, including industry concentration, the degree of sales promotion, overhead costs as a proportion of total costs, and the strength of trade unions.

Kaleckian and other post-Keynesian pricing models have firms set administered prices with the expectation of sales usually being below production capacity, whereas in pricing analysis in the previous section assumes full capacity utilisation. Firms operate with excess capacity to enable them to meet fluctuations in demand and to dissuade entrants. Fluctuations in demand for the industry's product therefore don't affect administered prices, avoiding the complication of oscillating investment and prices encountered when prices are market-determined.

Despite having a normal pricing routine based on full capacity operation, Metcalfe (1998, p. 93) concurs with the post-Keynesian treatment of fluctuating demand, stating, 'in the first instance, the impact of turbulent conditions will be reflected in departures from full capacity operation, in excess order books or unfilled capacity.' Demand fluctuations impact realised profits but there are no price oscillations in the analysis for administered prices in Section 5.2.2. Only expected demand growth impacts the growth of productive capacity determined by (5.16) and the administered price determined by the normal pricing routine in (5.17).

Linking of price determination to the internal financing of investment in Section 5.2.2 has parallels in post-Keynesian analysis by Eichner (1973, 1976 and 1985), Wood (1975), and Harcourt and Keynon (1976). In each case the firm administratively determines a price, taking account of both the positive impact of a higher price in providing finance for the expansion of production capacity and the negative impact of a higher price on consumer demand for its product. The distinctive features of each of these works and their links to the broader price theory literature are discussed in Melmiès (2022) and Bloch and Kriesler (2023).

Post-Keynesian pricing analysis generally doesn't deal directly with the phenomenon of differential firm growth. An exception is the analysis of Steindl (1976). Steindl analyses the pattern of competition driven by internal accumulation for an industry with heterogeneous firms. As in the evolutionary analyses of Nelson and Winter (1982) and Metcalfe (1998), Steindl has low-cost firms growing faster than high-cost rivals due their greater profits and investment through internal accumulation. With a persistent cost advantage, the low-cost firms grow faster than industry average leading to rising market shares, such as for the entrepreneurial firm in (5.1).

Steindl suggests the low-cost firms engage in aggressive price and selling competition to continue growing faster than the industry, which eventually drives many high-cost firms from the industry. When the share of high-cost firms becomes negligible, the low-cost firms recognise their collective interest in reducing aggressive competition and the growth of their productive capacity. After this, low-cost firms use high profits to pay off debt or increase returns to shareholders and management.[20]

Steindl's analysis is distinguished from the evolutionary analysis of differential firm growth in Section 5.2.2 by incorporating changes in investment and pricing routines of low-cost firms in response to rising industry concentration. Changes in pricing and investment behaviour are changes in routines, which are compatible with evolutionary analysis. Markey-Towler (2016) explores the constraint market demand imposes on firm growth and how the choice of pricing routine is related to this constraint. Almudi et al. (2020) consider the impact that consumer learning has on demand and how firms react by changing their pricing routines. Integrating changes in firm pricing routines into analysis of the evolution of industry structure is a useful direction for future research in evolutionary price theory.

5.4 Summary

An economy experiencing innovation-driven growth is an economy where prices are in motion. Current prices coordinate buyers and sellers, creating market order, while providing only imperfect guides to future prices on which the profitability of investments depend. Heterogeneity across producers is common, even for similar or identical products. Movements in prices over time reflect the outcome of the contest between rival producers with their different products, processes, and organisations, a contest heavily influenced by the institutional environment in which firms operate.

Under capitalism profits are a market test for firms. They also provide firms with access to finance for expansion. High profits mean firms with superior products, productivity, or organisation can demonstrate their fitness by expanding relative their inferior rivals. The two models of differential firm growth developed in this chapter show how cost heterogeneity translates into differential firm growth, price dynamics, and the evolution of industry structure. One model assumes individual firms are price takers, with price determined by the interaction of supply and demand in the market. The other model assumes firms set prices through administrative routines designed to balance the growth of their production capacity with the growth of demand for their product.

---

[20] Detailed discussion of Steindl's theory of industry concentration based on differential firm growth through internal accumulation is provided in Bloch (2005). Steindl's theory of competition is compared to that of Schumpeter in Bloch (2000).

Replicator dynamics relating the change in weighted average unit cost to the share-weighted covariance of firm cost differences and growth differences, as shown in (5.10), apply with both market-determined and administered prices. The covariance is negative with lower-cost firms growing faster, so weighted average unit cost declines over time. Balance between the growth of industry supply and demand means prices decline as weighted average unit cost declines, whether through administrative design or through coordination by market price.

Part III Macro
6 Price Linkages and Structural Change

In this chapter and the next, the analysis is broadened to consider influences that extend beyond the individual consumer or firm (micro level) or industry (meso level). Unlike mainstream economics with its microfoundations for macroeconomics, evolutionary analysis at the macro level is interdependent with analysis at the micro and meso levels. Roughly, this chapter deals with influences linking industries together, the flow of commodities across industries and the movement of firms between industries. Chapter 7 deals with influences that affect all industries in the economy, including waves of innovations that interact with monetary and financial mechanisms.

Prices are linked across industries through flows of raw materials and intermediate product, which are captured in the input-output analysis of Leontief (1986) or the analysis of production of commodities by means of commodities by Sraffa (1960). Both Sraffa and Leontief assume a single production process for each industry. Yet, evolutionary price theory recognises heterogeneity across firms as a driver of structural change in the economy. Thus, adaptation of inter-industry analysis of the flow of commodities is proposed to allow for firm heterogeneity while examining the connection of prices across industries.

Implications for firm and industry boundaries of restless knowledge and the self-transformative activities of firms, including firms moving across industry boundaries, are discussed in the next section. Section 6.2 discusses entry and exit of firms as an alternative to internal accumulation to accommodate industry growth and decline, while Section 6.3 is devoted to adapting inter-industry analysis for use in evolutionary price theory. Section 6.4 discusses price determination in the long period, while Section 6.5 summarises.

6.1 Boundaries of Firms and Industries

Analysis in Chapter 5 associates a firm with a particular market in competition with a group of firms that form an industry. Further, it is assumed each firm operates a single production process that expands or contracts at constant unit cost. All this is convenient for an analysis focusing on the market as a selection environment for competition among the heterogeneous group of firms in the industry, with creative destruction as the driver of industry evolution and price dynamics.

Diversifying into new markets or developing new products allows firms to continue internal accumulation without engaging in aggressive competition to increase their share of existing markets. Restless knowledge ensures a steady supply of new ideas, which may be captured as innovations by firms able to search, seize, and secure the opportunities. Teece (2024) argues this requires dynamic capabilities for going beyond established routines.

If firms are not confined to specific products or markets, what meaning remains for the concept of an industry? An answer starts with Marshall's (1920) analogy between firms in an industry and trees in a forest. There are both complimentary and competitive relationships among firms engaged in related activities. They share overlapping sets of customers and suppliers, as well as connections through industry associations, training colleges, specialised consultancies, and the like. Connections across a group of firms stronger than connections to firms outside the group define an industry.

Mainstream analysis has emaciated Marshall's analysis of the firm and its relationship to the industry. Pigou (1920) replaces Marshall's heterogeneous firms (trees in the forest) with the equilibrium firm, while Robinson (1931) insists the equilibrium firm is an optimising firm. Heterogeneity is ruled out.

Individuals and firms are at the core of evolutionary development, but not as the isolated economic agents assumed in methodological individualism. Non-market interactions are central to the process that leads to development by connecting the specialised knowledge of individuals through the exchange of information. As discussed in Chapters 2 and 3, these interactions occur in multiple contexts, including among individuals as consumers, between individuals within firms, among firms within industries. Firms and industries also have interactions with governments, universities, and other social organisations. Discussion in this section explores some of these interactions and their implications for understanding the changing boundaries of firms and industries.

6.1.1 Restless Knowledge

Individual knowledge is continually changing through experience and learning, as well as the more dramatic changes due to births and deaths. As noted in Chapter 2, these changes don't occur in isolation. Interactions between individuals are essential, starting from socialisation of new-borns through to the evolution of culture and institutions (Veblen 1899). Similarly, interactions among individuals within firms change the correlated understanding among those individuals that allows their specialist knowledge to be combined to generate innovation through new patterns of action (Bloch and Metcalfe 2011).

Restless knowledge replenishes variety among firms to offset the loss associated with diffusion of innovations through differential firm growth as analysed in Chapter 5. As Shackle (1970, p. 155, italics in the original) notes, 'The paradox of business, in its modern evolution, is the conflict between our assumption that we know enough for our logic to bite on, and our *essential*, prime dependence on achieving *novelty*, the novelty which by its nature and meaning in some degree discredits what had passed for knowledge.'

Turning changes in correlated understanding into the creative action of innovation requires overcoming resistance to change. Schumpeter ([1934] 1961) suggests a special style of leadership is needed, which he attributes to the entrepreneur cast as a heroic individual. Later, in Schumpeter ([1950] 1976), he extends the analysis to include institutionalisation of innovation within large firms. In addition to distinguishing between inventions as the manifestation of new knowledge and innovations as their implementation in the economy, Schumpeter argues new ideas aren't sufficient to guarantee a flow of innovations into the economy. Capitalism provides the institutionalised context in which enterprising firms convert restless knowledge into innovations.

6.1.2 Firm Growth and Dynamic Capabilities

Taking advantage of the specialist knowledge of individuals within the firm requires organisation, and organisation is the job of management. While Schumpeter distinguishes between management and entrepreneurship, Penrose (1959, p. 261) recognises the overlap in roles, at least for large firms, 'treated as administrative organizations free to produce any kind of product they find profitable'. Penrose combines coordinating current production and planning for future growth through diversification and innovation as tasks undertaken by management in large firms.

Penrose rejects the emaciated image of the firm as a static optimiser and follows Marshall in treating successful firms as growing and developing. She argues the role of management in planning for future growth limits the rate of growth obtainable. While firms can add more managers, integrating them into the correlated understanding required for effective functioning of the firm takes time and effort from current managers. Once integrated, the collective learning and experience of the management team enhances the ability of the firm to take on further growth. In this sense, there are economies from growth.

Emphasis on the firm's productive resources as the impetus to growth is further developed in literature on the resource-based view of the firm (Barney 1991) and on dynamic capabilities (Teece 2009). Firms acquire productive resources that are organised into administrative structures by management, which provide the firm with capabilities. These capabilities are deployed to take advantage of profitable opportunities involving current products and markets. They are also deployed to take the firm in the direction of diversification and innovation, providing the firm with sustainable competitive advantage (Porter 1985).

Teece (2024, p. 203) argues dynamic capabilities, 'are creative and insight-dependent components that cannot be routinized.' These components are provided by entrepreneurial managers who, 'are central to the firm's evolution because they have the ability to decide if existing capabilities will remain in the firm and whether new ones should be added' (Teece 2024, p. 205). Changing the capabilities of the firm is part and parcel of transforming the firm, so a firm with dynamic capabilities is a self-transforming firm epitomised in mega-firms, but possible in start-up, small, and large firms.

Mega-firms are organised for the continual evaluation of activities within and outside the firm, leading to sporadic reorganisation of the firm through merger, acquisition, divestment, and internal redeployment of resources. More generally, Bloch and Metcalfe (2011, p. 99) suggest, 'The ability to generate new products in the laboratories together with the deployment of managerial capabilities to related lines of business, as suggested by Penrose, mean that the innovating and enterprising firm can overcome the external limits associated with the size of individual product markets, which implies a theory of the firm in which growth and dominance are irresistible outcomes of the self transformation of innovating and enterprising firms.'

6.1.3 Boundaries of the Firm

Mainstream economics treats the boundaries of the firm as externally determined. Coase (1937) points to transaction costs as determining these boundaries. Essentially, firms face decisions to make or buy, with the dividing line determined to minimise cost. Internalised production is chosen if the cost is less than that of acquiring the item through a market transaction. Perfect information is not assumed and the cost of discovering prices is included in transaction cost.

Some fifty years later, Coase (1988, p. 47) acknowledges limitations to his analysis, 'if one is to explain the institutional structure of production in the system as a whole it is necessary to uncover the reasons why the cost of organizing particular activities differs across firms'. In an evolutionary analysis with emergent outcomes from dynamic capabilities, neither markets nor firms are fixed. Bloch and Metcalfe (2015) suggest innovations in the transmission and use of information have both lowered the costs of transactions through the market and raised the efficiency with which firms organise production internally. The division of activities between firms and markets that emerges, 'is historically specific, which helps to explain why different configurations are observed in different points of time and in different economies' (Bloch and Metcalfe 2015, p. 448).

The boundaries of a firm depend on the firm's history as well as on technology and institutions of the time and place. Expansion in the direction of existing activities is the path of least resistance given the specialised knowledge of the individuals in the firm and its established routines. However, competition in traditional markets can lead boundaries to change over time as the firm seeks out and exploits new markets for its existing products and services as well as developing new products and services. The make-or-buy decision is only one of many decisions defining the boundaries of the firm, all of which depend on its dynamic capabilities and the history of the opportunities that come to the firm's attention.[21] Firms differ because their histories differ.

6.1.4 Boundaries of the Industry

Growth of market demand constrains the collective expansion of the firms selling similar products. Firms diverting internal accumulation from existing products to new markets or products lessen the competitive pressure that leads to decreasing price in the analysis of Chapter 5. Balanced growth of market demand and production capacity may occur without further price reductions as in Steindl's (1976) model of industry maturity.

Diversification and product innovation blur the boundaries of an industry considered as a group of firms selling similar products. Marshall's (1920 and 1923) analysis of the complementary, as well as competitive, linkages among firms points to an alternative approach to defining industry boundaries, which

---

[21] See Kay (2018) for a critique of the mainstream approach to the theory of the firm based on transaction costs and hierarchical organisation, followed by an argument for shifting to a capabilities-based approach.

fits an evolutionary perspective that emphasises specialised knowledge and the incomplete flow of information between individuals. Bloch and Finch (2010, p. 142) note that Marshall 'argues that the economic basis of economic development is found among firms' relations with one another rather than within firms considered in isolation'. Marshall uses the imagery of an industrial college in the air that connects firms engaged in related economic activities. Proximity plays a role, as agglomeration economies are associated with industrial districts. Institutions are also important, such as industry associations, trade fairs, training colleges and universities, as is the use of common suppliers of equipment and materials.

The boundaries of industries are necessarily fuzzy and changing over time. Yet, the varying density of connections between firms across the economy provides a logic to classifying firms into clusters with relatively strong connections. The way firms organise themselves to exploit external connections is important. Any of the several points of contact between firms may provide the strongest connections. Thus, the appropriate classification criteria for grouping firms into industries vary.

Fuzzy industry boundaries mean the heterogeneity of firms classified into the industry tends to exceed the type of heterogeneity of unit cost dealt with in Chapter 5. Variety in products, marketing, or other characteristics across firms in the industry adds to variety in production processes.[22] Yet, if boundaries are carefully defined, there are closer connections among firms within the boundaries of an industry than to other firms in the economy. Such an industry provides a multi-dimensional selection environment for testing of the fitness of heterogeneous firms.

6.2 Entry and Exit

Structural change in terms of changes in the relative size of industries is a standard feature of evolving economies along with the creation of new industries and the disappearance of old industries. Sharply contrasting analyses of the relationship between firm size and industry size are provided by evolutionary and neoclassical economics. In the analysis of differential firm growth in Chapter 5, changes in industry size are accommodated through adjustment of existing firm sizes (fit firms growing and unfit firms stagnating or shrinking). No entry or exit of firms occurs. In neoclassical economics with long-run perfectly competitive equilibrium, changes in industry size occur through a change in the

---

[22] See Bloch (1981) for evidence of the role of cost differences, stochastic firm growth, and aggregation of markets for determining the variance of market shares in Canadian manufacturing industries.

number of firms, each firm operating at the same output level with price equal to minimum long-run average cost (ignoring problems associated with fractions of firms). No change occurs to the size of existing firms.

Entry and exit of firms are important phenomena and deserve to be analysed constructively in the theory of price determination, whether evolutionary or neoclassical. Sporadic attempts at a theory of entry by neoclassical economists over the years include Marshall's (1920) analysis of long-run supply based on the representative firm, models of barriers to entry by Bain (1956) and Sylos-Labini (1962), and game-theoretic models of firm strategy toward technology and marketing by Sutton (1991 and 1998). These attempts have been met by subversion (witness the fate of Marshall's representative firm), counterattack (for example, Baumol et al. (1982) attacking models of barriers to entry with the concept of contestable markets), and, mostly, indifference. Determining the amount of entry and exit into an industry by equating price to minimum average cost is an article of faith for the mainstream, rather than the result of a theory of entry.

Entry and exit of firms can be incorporated into the analysis in Chapter 5. Exit of firms is a straightforward extension. When industry price falls below a firm's unit cost, the firm's operating surplus (the gap between revenue and operating cost) is below depreciation charges and net investment is negative. If the firm's operating surplus is below its fixed expense (interest on loans, lease payments, and the like), it becomes insolvent. If price drops below operating cost per unit of output, production ceases even without fixed expenses.

Entry of firms is an indirect effect of differential firm growth when entry into new industries is an outcome of diversification efforts as discussed in Section 6.1.3. The presumption in Chapter 5 is that the knowledge and organisational capability required for operating in the industry is limited to existing firms. However, these obstacles to operating in the industry aren't insurmountable. Firms in the supply chain may diversify upstream or downstream using knowledge and capabilities from their network connections. Employees of existing firms are another source of new entrants, especially employees coming from low-cost firms.

An entrant's survival is far from assured. An immediate threat to its survival occurs if actual unit cost exceeds the expected level or actual price received is below expected price, leading to lower profits than anticipated. Afterward, new firms are exposed to the same competitive selection environment as existing firms. Unless the entrant's unit cost is near or below that of the lowest cost firms, falling prices due to high growth of the lowest cost firms eventually result in prices below the entrant's unit cost. Creative destruction is an existential threat to entrants and established firms alike.

Once an entrant commits its financial and organisational resources to an industry it is unlikely to be able to exit without experiencing a substantial loss on the value of these resources. The inability to exit without loss constitutes a barrier to entry for an industry experiencing creative destruction. Potential entrants into such an industry only enter if current average product price for the industry is substantially above the entrant's expected unit cost (Eaton and Lipsey 1980).

Metcalfe (1998) adds entry to the analysis of differential firm growth by assuming a potential supply of new firms. A firm enters only when industry price is at a minimum threshold above its expected unit cost. Expected unit cost is heterogeneous across the potential entrants, for reasons similar to those causing unit cost to differ across existing firms. Entry occurs at a finite rate that increases with the industry average price, as more firms find the price exceeds their threshold.

Entry modifies the dynamics associated with differential firm growth by existing firms. Entry adds to production and puts downward pressure on price. Profits of the existing firms are lower, which slows the growth of their production capacity. As Metcalfe (1998) argues, what matters to industry price and the dynamics of market shares of established firms is the share of industry sales taken by entrants as a group, which is generally small.

These observations about the drivers of entry and exit are far from providing a satisfactory theory. In the context of established industries, they are ancillary to the theory of differential firm growth in determining price dynamics. However, the entry process is fundamental for understanding the evolution of new industries, and this involves institutional and sociological influences as well as economic (see Gustafsson et al. 2016 for a discussion). Bloch (2018c) discusses both the mainstream and evolutionary economics literature on innovation and the evolution of industries.

6.3 Inter-industry Linkages

Industries are linked by the flow of products, as well as the flow of firms, across industry boundaries. When the output of one industry is used as an input by another industry, the revenues of the first industry are costs for the second. Price movements in input-supplying industries thus flow through to costs and prices throughout the economy. These linkages in price are discussed in Section 6.3.2. First, a mechanism is required for summarising the movement of unit cost and price within an industry when firms are heterogeneous, with the representative firm proposed as the mechanism.

6.3.1 The Representative Firm

Marshall (1920) uses the concept of a representative firm to separate the analysis of influences that are firm specific from the analysis of influences common to all firms in an industry. In Appendix H of Marshall (1920, pp. 664–669), this separation is applied in determining the shape of the long-run industry supply curve in an industry with increasing returns to scale. As industry output expands, average cost at the representative firm tends to fall due to common influences on all firms, such as cost reductions from improved supply chains, better trained labour, and enhanced specialist services. These external economies reflect the greater division of labour possible at greater industry size as well as common impacts of learning by doing. Average cost may also fall due to enhanced size of the representative firm, but only to the extent average firm size across the industry increases.

Marshall (1920, p. 265, apostrophes in original) suggests the representative firm 'is in a sense an average firm. But there are many ways in which the term "average" might be interpreted in connection with a business'. Marshall implies there is an actual firm or two that are close to matching the appropriate average and can be used as representative. However, this approach is problematic in two respects.

First, Marshall suggests individual firms are in flux, rising or falling, so it is unreasonable to expect an individual firm to remain average for very long. Flux suggests the position of a firm in the distribution of firm characteristics is continually subject to change. Second, as shown in the analysis of differential growth among firms with heterogeneous unit costs in Chapter 5, share-weighted averages of unit cost, price-cost ratio, and price shift over time, which occurs independently of change in unit cost at any firm. The average values associated with being representative change, meaning a firm that is representative in one period is not representative in the next.

Metcalfe (2007) identifies the second problem and proposes a solution, defining the representative firm by its relationship to the distribution of firm characteristics. Metcalfe's representative firm is a hypothetical firm that grows at the same rate as the industry. With competitive selection through differential firm growth and constant unit cost at each firm, the unit cost required for firm growth to equal industry growth falls as the distribution of market shares clusters around the low end of the unit-cost distribution. While no actual firm grows at the same rate as the market under these circumstances, a hypothetical firm with declining unit cost over time can match market growth.

Metcalfe's candidate for representative firm incidentally overcomes the first problem for Marshall's use of an actual firm as representative. A firm with constant market share has an average rate of growth for the industry, which means it is free from firm-specific influences that might cause an actual firm to become unrepresentative in terms of its growth rate. The same representativeness property applies to the representative firm defined as a firm with share-weighted average values of product price, unit cost, and price-cost ratio.[23] This definition fits with the analysis of Chapter 5, which shows how average values for unit cost, price and price-cost ratio move with the shifting distribution of market shares towards the firm with lowest unit cost.

The redefined representative firm is neither an optimal firm nor a best-practice firm. The optimal firm is an extreme of a theoretical distribution of firms, which is unlikely to exist in a world of imperfect knowledge. A best-practice firm is an extreme of the distribution of existing firms. With average values of key characteristics, the redefined representative firm is central to the distribution of these characteristics. Marshall understood the difference between average and optimal or best practice. He used the concept of the representative firm to capture this difference, a difference that proves useful in the following analysis.

6.3.2 Inter-industry Linkages in Prices

Industries are linked through the flow of intermediate products, with services, construction, and durable equipment being outputs of one industry and inputs to another. Input-output analysis developed by Leontief (1986) provides an empirical framework for linking production flows across industries. Neoclassical economics builds on this framework using Walrasian general equilibrium theory. However, as discussed in Chapter 4, equilibrium theory is inappropriate for use in evolutionary analysis as the requirements of optimising behaviour along with externally determined technology, preferences and resources are incompatible with analysing economic evolution.

Sraffa (1960) examines the requirements for reproduction in an economy where commodities are produced through combining commodities and labour. In the tradition of long-period analysis of classical economics, the price for each commodity is equal to its unit production cost calculated using the corresponding prices of all commodities used as inputs along with a uniform wage rate and rate of profits across commodities. Roncaglia (1978, p. 16, apostrophes in original) points to the omission of any requirement for equilibrium as a feature distinguishing Sraffa's analysis from neoclassical analysis, 'The fact

---

[23] Under Metcalfe's (2007) assumptions, this firm has a constant market share provided it also has an industry-average propensity to accumulate through investing profit in the expansion of production capacity.

Evolutionary Price Theory   65

that Sraffa never talks of an "economic equilibrium" or of "equilibrium prices" in relation to his system should also be emphasized.'

Sraffa shows for any given structure of technical requirements of commodity inputs and labour for producing each commodity there is a corresponding unique set of reproduction prices for any given wage rate or profit rate. There is also a monotonic inverse relationship between the wage rate (assuming homogenous labour) and the rate of profit. Thus, if one rate is set the value or the other is uniquely determined.

Roncaglia (2006) distinguishes three orientations by Sraffa scholars towards classical economics. First is the Ricardian reconstruction of Pasinetti (1981), second is the Marxian reconstruction of Garegnani (1990), and third is the Smithian reconstruction of Sylos-Labini (1984). Roncaglia (2006, p. 466) notes the Smithian approach has an advantage in terms of flexibility regarding prices and profits, 'while the notion of surplus retains a central role in economic analysis, the functional relationships connecting production prices and income distribution lose their role as the central pillar of economic theorising'.

Bloch (2018b) provides an evolutionary analysis of inter-industry linkages in prices using a modification of Sraffa's framework following a Smithian approach. The evolutionary analysis uses the following system of equations in matrix notation,

$$\mathbf{p} = \pi \mathbf{u} = ((\mathbf{I} - \pi \mathbf{A})^{-1})\pi \gamma \mathbf{w}, \tag{6.1}$$

where $\mathbf{p}$ is the vector of commodity prices (the ith element, p_i, is the price of the ith commodity), π is a diagonal matrix of price-cost ratios (only diagonal elements are non-zero and the ith diagonal element, π_{ii}, is the price-cost ratio for the ith industry, $\mathbf{u}$ is the vector of unit production cost for all commodities, $\mathbf{A}$ is the matrix of input-output coefficients, γ is the vector of labour requirements and $\mathbf{w}$ is the vector of share-weighted average wage rates, with elements of w_i. Elements of the matrix $\mathbf{A}$ give the share-weighted direct requirements for producing each commodity, where a_{ij} gives the direct requirements of commodity j used in producing one unit of commodity i. Elements of the vector, γ, give the share-weighted average direct labour requirement for producing each commodity, with elements of γ_i.

In adapting Sraffa's framework for evolutionary price theory, the vectors and matrices used in (6.1) are values for the redefined version of Marshall's representative firm rather than assuming a single production process applying to all producers as in Leontief (1986) or Sraffa (1960). In Section 6.1.5 the redefined representative firm has share-weighted average values of price, unit cost and the price-cost ratio. Implementing this interpretation in the system of equations in

(6.1) implies average unit cost is determined by share-weighted average technical coefficients and a share-weighted average wage rate for the industry, while the share-weighted average price equals this share-weighted average unit cost multiplied by the share-weighted average price-cost ratio.

Using the redefined representative firm with share-weighted average industry values of technical coefficients, price-cost ratio, and wage rate has the advantage that flows of revenues and cost add up across the economy. The system of equations in (6.1) is interpretable as a system of accounting relationships in which the price in each industry is equated to the average unit cost of production times an average price-cost ratio. This interpretation fits with the Smithian reconstruction of Sraffa as noted by Roncaglia (1978), although shifting the focus of analysis from long-period analysis of production prices and income distribution to the analysis of the trajectory of costs, profitability, and prices occurring in the process of creative destruction.[24]

Differential firm growth with creative destruction leads to changes in average technical coefficients, unit costs, price-cost ratios, and prices. These changes occur because of changing the market shares of producers, even without unit cost changing at individual producers. Diffusion and adaptation to major innovations occur over long periods of time, witness the decades taken for diffusion of railways, mass production of motor vehicles, or automation in food manufacturing.

As, and the word, price changes within an industry, the system of equations in (6.1) provides a framework for tracing impact throughout the economy.[25] Industries using inputs from an industry experiencing creative destruction are most directly impacted. If the product of the industry experiencing creative destruction is a basic commodity as defined by Sraffa, prices in all industries are impacted without any change in their wage rate or price-cost ratio. Otherwise, the range of affected industries is limited but extends beyond the initial industry, aside from the case of commodities that aren't used in the production of any other commodity. Quantities are affected as well as prices, with industries whose relative prices fall expanding and those with higher relative prices contracting as suggested by the analysis of orderly markets in Chapter 4.[26]

---

[24] Kurz (2008) examines the impact of innovations on long-period prices using a Sraffian framework with equalisation of wage rates across commodities and zero profit for all. Bloch (2018a and 2018b) discusses the relationship between Kurz's analysis and analysis focusing on the trajectory of costs and prices in the process of creative destruction.

[25] With a single market-determined price or with price leadership, each downstream industry pays the same price for its intermediate input. Otherwise, (6.1) only approximates the payments between industries.

[26] The stability properties of quantity and price outcomes in a Leontief or Sraffian framework with evolutionary analysis are discussed by Shiozawa, et al. (2019), Apromourgos et al. (2022), and Wang (2024).

6.4 Prices in the Long Run

A theory for determining prices in the long run has been the holy grail of economics.[27] Classical economic theory of natural prices relates the long-run relative price of a commodity to its cost of production. Ricardo ([1821] 1973) argues this means long-run relative prices approximate their relative labour content, including both direct and indirect labour. Marx ([1887] 1954) shifts focus slightly and argues long-run relative values depend solely on relative direct and indirect labour, but then has trouble converting long-run relative labour values into long-run relative prices.[28]

Sraffa (1960) uses the framework of production of commodities by means of commodities to clarify confusions of classical theory, including demonstrating an invariable standard of value in the form of the standard commodity. He also demonstrates the invariable standard of value is unique to each set of technical coefficients, so technical change, unless it is balanced across all commodities, changes the standard commodity. Thus, comparisons over time for economies experiencing structural change inevitably must be based on variable standards of value.

Neoclassical economists object to purely cost-based determination of prices in the long run, especially the notion that prices are determined by labour values. They argue unit cost generally depends on the scale of production, so demand as well as supply conditions affect relative prices in the long run. Also, they introduce marginal analysis for determining equilibrium prices. This has led to a theory of long-run relative prices based on intertemporal perfectly competitive general equilibrium with rational expectations. These prices are stable with respect to random disturbances. They only change with unexpected external influences. Very neat, but of questionable relevance for analysing an evolving economy, where prices are determined by endogenous processes of innovation and structural change.

Marshall (1920) introduces the representative firm in analysing long-run supply conditions for an industry, which he then combines with long-run demand conditions to determine long-run relative prices using his famous scissors analogy. The unit cost for the representative firm includes the cost of use of durable plant and equipment along with a normal return on invested capital. Marhsall argues entrants look to the representative firm as indicative of what they will experience after entry, with firms entering the industry whenever

---

[27] Bloch (2020) discusses the development of classical and neoclassical price theory, while Bloch (2022) extends the discussion to modern heterodox price theory.
[28] See Hunt (1979, Appendix to Chapter 10) for an introductory discussion of the problem of transforming values into prices.

price exceeds the unit cost of the representative firm. Firms exit whenever their unit cost is continuously below price. Marshall concludes the long-run supply price for an industry equals the unit cost for the representative firm.

Evolutionary price theory doesn't offer a theory of price in the long run as an equivalent to the natural price of classical theory, Marshall's long-run supply price, or the intertemporal general equilibrium price of modern neoclassical theory. Instead, it provides a theory of price determination in the process of the introduction and diffusion of innovations through creative destruction, which leads to a trajectory of prices over time. There are several important consequences.

First, rather than a fixed point or central tendency that market prices fluctuate around as in classical and neoclassical economics, there is a lower boundary to the trajectory of prices. Firm heterogeneity leads to differential firm growth and industry average price declines over time. In Chapter 5, the aspect of heterogeneity analysed is variation in unit cost, with the rate of price decrease depending on the variance of unit cost across firms. Without further innovation-induced changes in unit cost at the firm level, differential growth reduces variance of unit cost and the rate of price change declines over time as price approaches its lower boundary.

Second, evolutionary price theory occurs in historical time, not the logical time of classical or modern neoclassical price theory. The process of creative destruction is irreversible. It is also path dependent with stochastic events, such as innovation or entry of new firms, interrupting the decline in firm heterogeneity. Because innovation and entry are successful only to the extent that the entrant or innovator is fitter than average for the industry, they tend to enhance rather than reverse the downward trajectory of costs and prices.

Third, differential firm growth is driven by profit differentials across firms, with internal accumulation of the fittest firms driven by high relative profitability. The natural price in classical economics equals the unit cost of reproduction based on uniform profit and wage rates across firms. A uniform normal rate of return is included in both Marshall's long-run supply price that equals the unit cost of the representative firm and in neoclassical long-run perfectly competitive equilibrium price that equals minimum unit cost using best-practice technology. Profit in evolutionary price theory is driven by creative destruction, a degenerative process, rather than representing a payment for the use of capital as in classical and neoclassical price theory.

Fourth, the process of creative destruction takes time, more time than implied by Marshall (1920) in his distinction between short-run and long-run adjustment processes. Marshall associates the difference between the short and long runs with the time required to expand or contract production capacity to meet demand. The analysis is Chapter 5 presumes firms build capacity ahead of demand over the interval between periods. Yet, creative destruction continues indefinitely, limited by the speed with which the fittest firms can expand their market shares at the expense of less fit rivals. As the heterogeneity across firms declines, the speed of adjustment declines so heterogeneity disappears asymptotically at the infinite horizon. Innovation and entry add to variety and, thereby, interrupt the process of adjustment.

6.5 Summary

Part III focuses on aspects of evolutionary price theory that extend beyond an isolated consumer, firm, or industry. The emphasis in this chapter is on influences that link industries together, starting with restless knowledge. Restless knowledge generates opportunities for innovation that extend beyond traditional boundaries of the firm and industry. Firms with dynamic capabilities exploit these opportunities, making industry boundaries porous in an evolving economy.

Entry and exit of firms affect the dynamics of market shares and prices in industries undergoing creative destruction, which impacts results from the analysis of differential firm growth in Chapter 5. Except for new industries, the impact is unlikely to be substantial due to the small share of industry output accounted for by entrants or exits. A theory of entry and exit suitable for evolutionary analysis is a work in progress.

Price changes spread through the economy through the flow of products between industries. For purposes of tracing these impacts, the industry is represented by a firm with share-weighted average values of technical production coefficients, wage rate, unit cost, price-cost ratio, and price. A system of equations with these representative firm values for each industry provides the mechanism for calculating the direct and indirect impacts of changes in the price for the representative firm in one industry on costs and prices for representative firms in all other industries.

Evolutionary price theory is a theory of the movement of prices through time rather than a theory of the structure of prices in the long run as in classical and neoclassical economics. Prices move with the process of differential firm growth. The process occurs slowly over time, is irreversible and path dependent. The process is degenerative, with shrinking market shares of unfit firms consuming the heterogeneity that drives differential firm growth. However, entrepreneurial action based on restless knowledge, creativity, and imagination ensure variety is replenished and development from within continues indefinitely.

7 Waves of Innovation and Price Movements

The whole is more than the sum of the parts in evolutionary price theory, which is clearly apparent when it comes to movements in the aggregate price level. Analysis in Chapter 5 shows how price movements at the industry level are driven by differential firm growth, while analysis in Chapter 6 shows how price changes in one industry feed through unevenly to unit cost and prices in other industries. Schumpeter adds a macro-level analysis that links waves of innovation to movements in the level and structure of prices across the economy.

Innovation drives economic growth in Schumpeter's ([1934] 1961) *Theory of Economic Development*. Innovation requires action from entrepreneurs to overcome resistance to change. Entrepreneurs are distinguished by their imagination and leadership rather than their control over production. Implementing innovations requires obtaining means of production in competition with established producers, which tends to drive up prices of means of production for all producers. Once in production, the output from innovators competes with established products, tending to drive down prices for all products by varying amounts.

Schumpeter argues money is not simply a veil for barter transactions. Financing of innovation through bank credit means changes in innovation activity are inextricably linked to movements in the money supply. The money supply is endogenous due to the expansion and contraction of credit to finance innovation, which strengthens the connection between innovation intensity and inflation.

The links between movements in prices and the intensity of innovation are further developed in Schumpeter's (1939) *Business Cycles*. Unevenness over time in the intensity of innovation is attributed to an endogenous feedback process between innovations and the reliability of price information. Reliable price information, which Schumpeter associates with prices being at normal levels, makes it possible for entrepreneurs to accurately calculate the profitability of innovations. An upsurge in innovative activity is encouraged. However, the diffusion of these innovations through creative destruction disrupts markets. Then, information conveyed by current prices isn't a reliable indicator of future prices, which means innovative activity is discouraged.

Schumpeter's macro-level analysis is the foundation for the theory of aggregate price movements developed in this chapter, albeit with modifications made to overcome flaws in Schumpeter's arguments. Modifications are also made to incorporate aspects of the micro- and meso-level analyses of previous chapters, and to accommodate historical changes in the institutional environment since Schumpeter's time. Order and disruption remain counterpoints in the theory.

Financing of innovations and the implications for movements in the aggregate price level are discussed in the next section. Section 7.2 discusses the theory of waves of innovation. Section 7.3 combines the macro analysis of the price level with analysis at the micro and meso levels to demonstrate the limitations of aggregate indexes and other aggregate measures in understanding development under capitalism.

7.1 Entrepreneurs, Credit, and Inflation

Entrepreneurs are essential to Schumpeter's theory of innovation-driven growth. They are distinguished by their imagination and by their sociological character of leadership, seeing opportunities invisible to others and convincing others of the viability of their vision. Bankers are also essential as entrepreneurs don't own means of production and require cooperation from bankers to finance their innovations.

Schumpeter ([1934] 1961, Chapter 3) notes his theory of economic development, with its emphasis on structural change through entrepreneurship, leads him to a heretical position on the role of credit and money. In particular, he rejects the view that money is a veil with no real influence on the course of economic development. Instead, the creation of credit that expands the money supply is necessary for entrepreneurs to acquire the means of production, diverting these inputs from established firms for use in innovative production activities.[29]

Schumpeter's heresy on credit and money extends to his treatment of capital. Schumpeter (1939, p. 129) treats capital 'as an accounting concept – as measuring in terms of money the resources entrusted to a firm'. Bankers serve as social accountants and gatekeepers through their granting of credit to entrepreneurs. Projects that are deemed able to return principal and interest are funded and become capital.

How can it be that financing innovation generates capital even though there are no additional means of production, only a shift of means of production from established producers to innovators? Innovation is an out-of-equilibrium process. The value of the innovation derives from the surplus between the stream of future revenues from sale of the innovative product and the stream of costs, including expenditures on the initial means of production and subsequent expenditures. For a successful innovation, this surplus exceeds the surplus that would have been obtained from the use of the means of production by

---

[29] Schumpeter ([1934] 1961, p.106) notes, 'in so far as credit cannot be given out of the results of past enterprise or in general out of reservoirs of purchasing power created by past development, it can only consist of credit means of payment created ad hoc, which can be backed neither by money in the strict sense nor by products already in existence.'

established producers. Thus, the value of the capital generated by financing innovation is validated ex post by the ability of entrepreneurs to repay banks with interest and still obtain profits. If the innovation fails to meet this market test, the entrepreneur is liquidated, the bank suffers a loss, and the capital is invalidated.

Schumpeter (1939, p. 123) defines interest in purely monetary terms: 'Interest is a premium on present over future means of payment.' He argues neither abstinence nor roundabout production is required to explain interest. Instead, entrepreneurial profits provide a logically sound, albeit transitory, source to pay interest. Interest is in a sense a tax paid by entrepreneurs to banks for obtaining access to means of production in advance of owning a share of society's resources. With innovations fully absorbed at the end of the business cycle, entrepreneurial profits are zero. Nothing is left with which to pay interest, so interest logically equals zero in a stationary state.[30]

The credit banks extend to entrepreneurs adds to the flow of expenditure in the economy, especially expenditure on the means of production, including labour, raw materials, and durable equipment. Prices of the means of production rise, increasing production cost for new and established producers alike. Wages rise, with these increased costs passed through to increased prices for intermediate and final products as indicated in the analysis of Section 6.3.2. The aggregate price level as measured by an index of weighted elements in the price vector then rises.[31]

Inflation associated with an upsurge in innovations is temporary. Schumpeter has entrepreneurs using profits from successful innovations to repay their loans. When entrepreneurs repay their loans, money supply falls as does aggregate nominal income, a process Schumpeter calls autodeflation. Additional output from the entrepreneurs more than replaces the output lost from established producers, so prices fall on average, contributing to falling nominal income.[32] Thus, Schumpeter concludes that there is a downward trend for the price level over the long period.

---

[30] The most extensive discussion of Schumpeter's theory of money, interest, and prices is contained in his unfinished and posthumously published *Treatise on Money* (Schumpeter 2014).

[31] Prices of services of durable means of production also increase. These services aren't included in the input-output matrix of (6.1), which includes only current inputs. Instead, increased prices of these services required to achieve market clearing in the short run appear as higher price-cost ratios for high-demand products. Bloch (2018a, Chapter 6) examines price determination in an evolving economy with durable capital goods explicitly included in the input-output matrix.

[32] Nominal income falling in tandem with the money supply is consistent with the quantity theory of money, but the causality implied by Schumpeter differs. Rather than the money supply contraction causing downward pressure on demand and prices, the fall in money supply and nominal income are both the result of the evolutionary process of repayment of loans as explained in Bloch (2018a, Chapter 5).

Minsky (1990), Knell (2015), and Callegari (2018) argue changes in the financial market institutions mean the simple relationship between credit and innovation posited by Schumpeter's analysis needs updating to explain cyclical behaviour in a modern economy. Schumpeter ([1950] 1976) acknowledges the start of this institutional shift, noting the enhanced role of large corporations in the innovation process. A large corporation shifting means of production from an established line of business to an innovative activity doesn't require access to external finance, nor does its innovative activity necessarily impact wage rates. Still, expansion of the innovative activity requires displacing established production and disruption of markets, except in the unlikely event that the large corporation is cannibalising its own markets. Thus, the inflationary and deflationary effects of credit expansion and contraction may be avoided, while the downward pressure on the price level over the long period remains.

Further discussion of Schumpeter's analysis of movements in the price level is postponed to Section 7.3. There, flaws in Schumpeter's explicit and implicit assumptions about micro-level behaviour and meso-level adjustment processes are identified and an integrated framework for analysing movements in prices across the economy is presented. First, the existence of long waves in the intensity of innovative activity and the links between these waves and the reliability of price information is considered in the following section.

7.2 Waves of Innovation

As discussed in Chapter 5, the intensity of innovation activity is tied to the reliability of price information in Schumpeter's endogenous process of growth and structural change. When current price information provides a reliable guide to future prices, entrepreneurs can accurately calculate the profitability of potential innovations and obtain credit from banks to finance those innovations. Innovations and their diffusion through creative destruction disrupt markets, making price information less reliable and further innovations are discouraged.

Feedback between the reliability of price information and the intensity of innovation is at the core of Schumpeter's theory of the business cycle. Reliable price information leads to a wave of innovations, a wave of innovations increases price growth but disturbs the price system. Uncertainty about future prices depresses innovative activity. Low innovative activity stabilises output and prices, reducing uncertainty about future prices. Repetition of the sequence over time creates waves of innovative activity that are the driving force of cycles in price and output growth.

The analysis in Chapter 5 relates the rate of price adjustment to the variance of cost differentials across producers. If the variance of cost differentials were known, insert, an estimate of, the rate of price adjustment consistent with the adjustment process could be calculated. However, this type of information is unlikely to be available to market participants. Also, as Steindl's (1976) analysis of price adjustment to cost differentials demonstrates, the price adjustment process may be erratic, with periods of price stability interspersed periods of intense price competition. The price of computer processing power has fallen dramatically over recent decades, but the rate of decline has been far from steady.

Price adjustments in a single industry spread through the economy in the analysis in Chapter 6. Price adjustments directly impact downstream industries through the price of intermediate inputs in the input-output matrix in (6.1). Entry and exit of firms may also impact prices through changes in price-cost margins in affected industries. Structural changes in the shares of various industries in aggregate production occur in tandem with changes in the structure of prices for individual industries.

The unknown dynamics of product prices in industries undergoing diffusion of innovations together with uneven pass through to cost and prices in other industries create uncertainty regarding the difference between cost and revenue for production processes throughout the economy. The sporadic nature of the process of entry and exit adds to uncertainty. Uncertainty of this sort may not have great impact on investments by established firms in their ongoing activities because they have ongoing commitments to employees, leases, loans, and customers. However, entrepreneurs who require access to external finance have difficulty developing business plans that avoid unacceptable uncertainty for their financiers.

Schumpeter's (1939) *Business Cycles* expands the business cycle theory beyond the primary cyclical activity. Innovative activity induces secondary expansion in non-innovating industries. This secondary expansion depends on boom conditions to be profitable, which disappear when innovative activity declines. Also, euphoria in the boom leads to banks extending credit to speculators, which means a downturn in innovative activity results in financial crisis as well as liquidation of unsustainable secondary expansion. Secondary phenomena add phases of depression and recovery to Schumpeter's original two phases of prosperity and recession.

Schumpeter bases the duration of the longest business cycle on a historical analysis of periods of innovation-driven growth in the world economy, settling on a length of fifty to sixty years in line with the work the Kondratieff (1935). He provides beginning and end dates for two long cycles, the Industrial Revolution from 1787 to 1842 and Railroadization from 1843 to 1897, as well as a beginning date, 1898, for a third long cycle of Electrification. He adds shorter cycles of about nine years duration due to the time taken to set up new industrial plant and equipment, Juglar cycles, and inventory cycles of about three years duration, Kitchin cycles. Then he suggests all cycles overlap if the Juglar cycles are 38 months (three and sixth years), the Juglar cycles are 114 months (9 and a half years), and Kondratieff cycles are 57 years in length.

Schumpeter's (1939) *Business Cycles* received mixed reviews. Economic historians were generally positive (Innis 1940, Rosenburg 1940). However, economists tended to be critical, with Kuznets (1940), a leading business-cycle analyst of the time, commenting unfavourably on the relationship between the theoretical model and the empirical content. Bloch (2018a, Chapter 3) provides a detailed discussion of Schumpeter's business cycle theory and the reactions it evoked.

Despite the critiques and lack of immediate adherents to Schumpeter's explanation for Kondratieff cycles in innovative activity, his notion that the frequency and impact of innovations follows a wave-like pattern over time has been gaining popularity (Tylecote 1992, Freeman and Louçã 2001, Perez 2002, Lipsey et al. 2005, Louçã 2021). While these advocates of waves of innovation generally cite Schumpeter as their inspiration, they tend to emphasise technological, financial, or institutional foundations for the wave-like movement. In doing so, they overlook Schumpeter's distinction between invention and innovation. They also overlook the endogenous mechanism involved when reliable price information helps overcome the barriers to turning inventions into innovations.

The connection between waves in innovative activity and movements in prices suggested by Schumpeter occurs regardless of the causal mechanism explaining the waves. Whether or not the reliability of price information is the cause of an upsurge in innovation, innovations require the shift of means of production from established producers to innovators and then the shift of expenditure from the products of established firms to those of the innovators. As Hayek (1935) explains, the price mechanism is key to these structural changes in inputs and outputs across the economy.

7.3 Movements in the Price Level and Price System

Schumpeter (1939) distinguishes between the price level and the price system. The price system refers to the relation of prices of individual products to each other, which is the subject of analysis in Chapter 6. For Schumpeter, the price level is a social construct relating the standard unit of account (money) to the full array of consumer expenditures. Schumpeter (1939, p. 454) warns, 'It is also easy to see that changes in the level can in practice hardly ever come about except by way of changes in the price system – even as changes in the system in practice hardly ever come about without enforcing a change in the price level.'

7.3.1 Changes in the Price System with Waves of Innovation

Analysing the impact of innovation waves on prices illustrates the difficulties of disentangling changes in the price level from changes in the price system. Schumpeter argues increasing innovation activity increases the prices of means of production, labour, raw materials, and capital equipment. Only the wage appears explicitly in the system of price-determining equations in (6.1). When the wage rate rises in (6.1), prices increase for all commodities that directly or indirectly use labour. However, the extent of the rise depends on the intensity of use of labour, which is unlikely to be uniform. If wage rates differ across commodities, they may well rise at different rates.

In the context of the system of price-determining equations, (6.1), raw materials and capital equipment are produced means of production. The cost of production for these commodities rises with wage rate increases. Additionally, price-cost ratios for these inputs tend to increase with greater demand, leading to rising prices relative to those of consumer goods.

In the case of raw materials, producers tend to behave as price takers as explained in Section 3.3.1. Price-taker firms generally find it most profitable to continually produce at full capacity. Changes in output for the individual firm don't affect prices, so there is no incentive to restrain output unlike price-maker firms who are limited in how much they can sell without lowering prices. With production at full capacity, any increase in market demand invariably leads to an increase in the price required for achieving market order as explained in Section 4.2. For Kondratieff cycles occurring from the seventeenth century through the early 2000s, the average price of primary commodities used as raw materials in manufacturing rises and falls with the cycle more than does the average price of manufactured goods (Bloch and Sapsford 2013).

Suppliers of capital equipment generally face downward sloping demand curves for their products and behave as price makers, setting administered prices as explained in Section 3.3.2. Some products are standardised but often they are made to order or at least modified to meet the requirements of the buyer, such as with airlines buying new aircraft. Producers don't maintain inventories, relying instead on order backlogs to manage fluctuating demand.

Price-cost ratios for capital equipment are not normally affected by fluctuations in demand. However, the discounts or premiums associated with modifications of product to meet buyer requirements are subject to negotiation and may well be impacted by fluctuations in market demand. More importantly, capital equipment is durable. Prices of used equipment are generally determined by negotiation or in second-hand auction markets, where demand fluctuations lead to price changes in the same direction to achieve market order. Thus, the average price-cost ratio in transactions for capital equipment, both new and used, is expected to rise with increased demand due to an upsurge in innovative activity. Anecdotal evidence supports this proposition, but the data needed for comprehensive testing are not available.

Differences in the ups and downs of prices across commodities over the course of Kondratieff cycles are large but pale in comparison to differences across commodities in trend movement. As explained in Section 3.4, prices of novel products generally decline rapidly relative to substitute goods and services, particularly over the adoption phase of the meso trajectory following their introduction. Over the course of the twentieth century prices of motor vehicles, television sets, computers, mobile phones, and internet services all have dropped dramatically in the decades of their adoption phases, even more so when adjusted for quality improvements.

Innovations also have impacted prices of established products. Mechanisation, irrigation, the Green Revolution in plant varieties, and other innovations have vastly increased production of many crops, outstripping the impact on demand of rising world population. As a result, the prices of agricultural products, such as wheat, rice, sugar, and cotton, have each dropped dramatically relative to many other prices.[33]

7.3.2 Aggregation in an Evolving Economy

Changes in the price level are usually measured through the movement of aggregate price indexes. Schumpeter (1939) cautions this provides at best an approximation. In a simple hypothetical case where the quantity of each item remains constant between two periods, the ratio of expenditure levels between the two periods unambiguously gives the ratio of price levels. Schumpeter extends this simple case by defining the change in the price level to be the change in consumer expenditure necessary to buy the same quantities of goods, which is equal to the Laspeyres price index with expenditure shares given by base-period price and quantity for each commodity. He adds there is little difference in using Paasche price index (with weights given by expenditure shares in the end period) or Fisher's ideal price index (with weights given by the

---

[33] Over the full length of the Kondratieff cycle spanning the trough of 1932 to the trough of 1993, the world price of wheat, rice, sugar, and cotton each fell at more than 1 per cent per annum relative to the average price of a basket of manufactured goods (Bloch and Sapsford 2013). A fall of 1 per cent per annum over sixty-one years basically cuts the relative price of these items in half.

average of expenditure shares in the beginning and end periods) if the changes in quantities over time are small.

Extending the comparison of price levels to longer periods is problematic in an evolving economy because the disparate changes in price across commodities noted earlier combine with structural change in the composition of output. Structural changes in relative importance of commodities result from waves of innovation under capitalism. For example, consumer expenditures were concentrated on food at the start of the Industrial Revolution, but the food share of expenditure by the typical household has declined as economies developed. Within the food category, expenditures have shifted from flour to baked goods, and then to restaurant and takeaway meals. Prices of flour, baked goods, and meals away from home have changed relative to each other and relative to the prices of all other goods. Thus, deflating nominal magnitudes by an aggregate price index with weights based on the initial share of consumer expenditures (a Laspeyres index) gives a different answer than deflation with an index based on the final share of consumer expenditure (a Paasche index).

Chain-link price indexes divide long periods into an overlapping series of shorter periods. The weights are fixed within each sub-period, but they change between sub-periods to reflect the changing pattern of expenditure. Inflation as measured by a chain-linked index within each short sub-period comes close Schumpeter's concept of the change in the price level. However, over long periods, the appearance of continuity provided by chain-link price indexes is undermined by changes in the pattern of weights. Changes in expenditure on a changing basket of commodities aren't separable into a change in average price and a change in average quantity in a way that is independent of the weighting system used in averaging.

The search for a way of separating changes in expenditures into changes in quantities and changes in prices goes back to the classical economists. They sought an invariable standard of value for use in examining the performance of economies over long periods of time, measured in terms of the magnitude of national output and the standard of living provided by the average wage. Smith ([1776] 1937) rejects precious metals as providing a standard arguing they are subject to fluctuations in price with new discoveries of metals. He presents data suggesting the absence of trend in the price of wheat over long periods but rejects wheat as a standard of value due to the short-run price impact of variable harvests.

Sraffa (1960) demonstrates that for any production structure of the type represented by matrix **A** in (6.1), there exists a composite commodity, which he calls the standard commodity, whose price is unaffected by changes in the wage rate or price-cost margin for the case where the wage ratio and price-cost ratio are uniform across industries. Thus, the standard commodity has some of the properties sought in an invariable standard of value. However, any change to technical coefficients in **A** (aside from proportional changes in all coefficients) cause the composition of the standard commodity to change. Thus, the standard commodity doesn't provide the type of invariable standard of value sought by classical economists because its own composition is variable.

Mainstream economists ignore the theoretical issues raised by Sraffa's critique. They treat the long run as the cumulation of a series of short runs, so are unworried about the adding up problem caused by structural change in the composition of aggregate output. When theorising about economic growth, they focus on steady-state growth models with perfect competition ensuring all producers are identical and structural change is absent. Such an analysis gives the appearance of dealing with growth and development but doesn't address Schumpeter's critique that growth under capitalism is driven by innovation and necessarily involves structural change and disparate price movements across commodities.

Evolutionary price theory as presented in this Element demonstrates the essential role of disparate price movements across commodities following a wave of innovations. Structural changes to the economy to accommodate the innovations require changes to the price system. Aggregation obscures these changes, thereby detracting from understanding the process of economic development under capitalism. Aggregation is unhelpful and is unnecessary in evolutionary price theory.[34]

7.3.3 Movements in the Price Level with Waves of Innovation

If Schumpeter's argument that growth under capitalism is driven by innovation and structural change is accepted, aggregate price indexes need be rejected as measures of the price level. Instead, the pattern of movements in prices across all commodities is what should be assessed. As noted in Section 7.3.1, changes in the price system due to the upsurge in a wave of innovations increase wage rates, as well as price-cost ratios for raw materials and for capital equipment. The price vector on the right-hand side of the system of equations for price determination in (6.1) increases. Disparate levels of increase in the prices of various commodities mean the size of the increase in any aggregate price index

---

[34] Almudi et al (2020) generalise the results from Chapter 5 by showing one very simple type of pricing routine is the first-order Taylor expansion of a large set of price-mechanisms. Moreover, that specific routine can be used without dispensing from agent heterogeneity in the models, thereby overcoming the lack of information in aggregate price indexes (which hides the coordinating role of heterogeneous prices).

depends on the weights given to each commodity. However, when the price of every final commodity is higher, the price level is unambiguously higher.

Following a wave of innovations, successful entrepreneurs use their extra profits to expand relative to non-innovating rivals, Analysis in Chapter 5 shows creative destruction from differential firm growth lowers price across all firms in the industry. With creative destruction leading to divergent price changes across industries, the change in an aggregate price index depends on the weight given to each price change. Some indexes may rise while others fall. The price level is a social construct, so determining the direction of change in the price level requires examining how disparate price changes impact all groups in society.

Disparate price movements across commodities in disrupted markets following a wave of innovations create confusion about the current and future price level. Entrepreneurs are not able to confidently predict the profitability of further innovations, which creates difficulties in obtaining finance from external sources. Innovation subsides and upward pressure on input prices abates, especially for prices of raw materials.[35] While some prices are likely to fall, overall economic conditions need not change sufficiently to drive down most prices and provide a definitive fall in the price level.

Discussion in Section 7.1 suggests trend in the price level over the full course of a wave of innovations depends on institutional arrangements for the financing of innovations. Trend movements in wage rates are also important, and they depend crucially on institutions and politics.[36] Disparate price movements along with structural change in consumption baskets make deflating a wage rate by an aggregate price index problematic as a way of determining the course of the real wage rate over such long periods of time. Likewise, deflating current expenditure on all final output produced in an economy by an aggregate price index hides the complex pattern of increases and decreases in the output of individual products. Real GDP is a very unreal concept.

Emphasis on the movement of economic aggregates and averages in mainstream economics diverts attention from the crucial role of structural change in economic development. Aggregate price indexes hide movements in relative prices, while aggregate output measures hide changes in the composition of output. Average wage movements hide the differential impacts of innovation, as

---

[35] Bloch and Sapsford (2004) provide evidence on the procyclical behaviour of commodity price and wage rates in the United States during the twentieth century. The procyclical movement of primary commodity prices with world industrial growth is identified as the key variable driving movements in the US producer price index.

[36] Evolutionary economists haven't addressed the determination of wage rates. However, there is a large post-Keynesian and political economy literature on the role of institutional and political factors in wage determination. See Lavoie (2022, Chapter 8) for a discussion of this literature.

do movements in average income or wealth. Evolutionary price theory employs a micro-meso-macro methodology, which permits analysis of disparate outcomes that development implies at the individual, industry, regional, or national level.

7.4 Summary

Motion, rather than equilibrium, is at the core of understanding movements in economic aggregates in a developing economy. Schumpeter identifies waves of innovation as the driving force behind growth and development in capitalist economies. Associated with these waves of innovation are movements in the price system and the price level. The price system is altered through changes in relative prices, the structure of production, and the pattern of consumer expenditure. Aggregate price indexes obscure changes in the price level due to the changing price system, undermining meaningful quantitative comparisons over long periods for aggregate output, the real wage, and the material standard of living.

Mainstream theory is presented as providing a logically consistent framework for economic analysis, including the analysis of economic change. Sraffa (1960) demonstrates there is no invariable standard of value for making logically consistent comparisons of prices when production processes are changing, which invalidates comparisons of aggregate output except for the case of steady-state growth. Steady-state growth with an unchanging production structure is implausible for an evolving economy. Mainstream price theory sweeps these contradictions under the carpet.

8 Summary and Topics for Further Research

8.1 Summary

The theory of price determination outlined in this Element is designed to be consistent with presumptions of evolutionary economic analysis. These presumptions include an open-system ontology in contrast to neoclassical economics with its closed-system ontology. Also, the constructed theory is based on co-evolution of micro, meso, and macro elements, which contrasts to the methodological individualism underpinning the microfoundations approach of mainstream economics. Further, the theory incorporates endogenous structural change with historical specificity and path dependence, contrasting to universality and time reversibility in mainstream economics.

Schumpeter's work on economic development is foundational to the evolutionary theory of price determination. To this are added ideas from evolutionary, behavioural, and post-Keynesian economists on the rules and routines used by consumers and firms. Marshall's analysis provides a framework for analysing the relationship between firms and industries, especially in orderly markets. Evolutionary and post-Keynesian analyses of differential firm growth provide guidance for the theory of price determination in disrupted markets. Inter-industry linkages of prices are built upon the work of Sraffa on production of commodities by means of commodities.

In Chapter 2, consumers are assumed to behave according to rules or routines, which contrasts to the optimising behaviour assumed in mainstream economics. Following rules or routines is a reasoned reaction to the limited cognition of decision makers, who are faced with incomplete information about the present and uncertainty regarding the future in an ever-changing economy. Habitual consumer behaviour contributes to inertia in market demand for mature products, while resistance to new products implies gradual diffusion along meso-trajectories shaped by market institutions and social networks.

Chapter 3 discusses pricing behaviour by firms. As with consumers, incomplete information and uncertainty lead to behaviour based on rules and routines, rather than optimisation. In addition, large firms face the task of coordinating the activity of substantial numbers of individuals with highly specialised knowledge, which makes establishing internal and external connections a primary focus of firm strategic planning. Heterogeneity among firms is highlighted, with differences in firm size, scope, organisation, and orientation discussed.

Heterogeneity in firm characteristics combines with heterogeneity in their historical experiences to lead to heterogeneity in pricing behaviour. Price-taker behaviour tends to occur when firms are small relative to the markets in which they operate, especially with organised trading exchanges. Price-maker behaviour occurs when firms have limited numbers of close competitors due to either large size relative to their markets or the differentiation of their products. Price leadership, which is useful for coordinating price behaviour among heterogeneous firms, involves aspects of price-taking behaviour (for price followers) and price-making behaviour (for price leaders). Pricing routines change with industry development, as exemplified by the pricing trajectories of novel products.

Chapter 4 explains the use of the concepts of coordinating price and market order to replace the mainstream concepts of equilibrium price and quantity. Equilibrium is inconsistent with the potential for change from within, which is an essential element of evolutionary analysis. Market order is achieved when bids from potential buyers are closely balanced with offers from potential sellers. In a market with undifferentiated products and numerous buyers and sellers, perfect market order is achieved with all transactions completed that involve bids equal or above the coordinating price and offers equal or below the coordinating price. Administered prices are coordinating prices for markets with heterogeneous products or small numbers of suppliers, with firms holding excess capacity to achieve market order.

Coordinating prices change when external influences cause variations in the bids or offers, much as shifts in supply and demand change the equilibrium price in mainstream price theory. However, the coordinating price also changes due to endogenous processes, such as the process of differential firm growth analysed in Chapter 5. As low-cost firms expand their production capacity relative to their high-cost rivals, more product is offered at low prices. With a homogenous product and price-taker firms, the coordinating price declines as shown in Figure 3. With differentiated products and administered prices, the share-weighted averages across firms of unit cost and prices decline as indicated in (5.21) and (5.19), respectively.

Analysis of price determination in Chapters 4 and 5 demonstrates the dual role of prices and markets in the evolutionary process of organisation and transformation in capitalist economies. Establishing market order is an example of the organising role of prices, while differential firm growth is an example of the transformational role of prices. Prices provide information to buyers and sellers to complete mutually beneficial transactions, while prices combine with heterogeneous costs to finance differential firm growth leading to change in industry structure. Prices contribute to both the self-ordering of capitalist economies and to their self-transformation.

The transformational role of prices also involves providing information to entrepreneurs to identify profitable opportunities for innovation. Heterogeneous expectations or imaginings of the future are an essential driver of endogenous change. Reliable information on current and future prices enhances the confidence in calculating the potential profitability of innovations for both entrepreneurs and their prospective financiers. Realised profitability is the outcome of the market testing of divergent expectations and imaginings. No one knows the future and assuming otherwise is a nonsense, as is assuming that expectations are correct on average.

Chapter 6 discusses fuzzy boundaries for firms and industries. Restless knowledge presents opportunities for innovation both within and outside established firms. Entrants with new processes and products enter established industries or create new industries, provided they have access to finance. Boundaries of firms and industries are changeable when firms exploit innovations in multiple markets, or when diversification offers a strategy for firm growth while avoiding aggressive competition in existing markets. Dynamic capabilities enhance the ability of firms to move into new markets and industries, with mega-firms institutionalising the development of dynamic capabilities to achieve sustainable competitive advantage through self-transformation of the firm.

Chapter 6 also discusses inter-industry linkages in prices from an evolutionary perspective. Rather than assuming a single best-practice technique in each industry, evolutionary analysis incorporates the impact of firm heterogeneity. A hypothetical firm with industry-average values of input requirements, price-cost margins, and prices is used to represent the industry. Creative destruction through differential firm growth leads to declines in unit cost, price-cost margin, and price for the representative firm, even without further technological change at any firm in the industry.

Price decreases spread through the economy as input costs decrease for firms in downstream industries. Importantly, the whole process of price adjustment is an example of evolutionary change. As the process reduces heterogeneity, the rate of change slows. However, the introduction of novelty through entrepreneurial action based on restless knowledge, imagination and creativity ensures continued development from within. Long-run equilibrium is a nonsense. There is a journey, but the destination keeps changing before it is reached.

The micro-meso-macro methodology of evolutionary price theory features in Chapter 7, which discusses movements in economic aggregates in a developing economy. Schumpeter argues waves of innovation have a macro impact, generating cycles in prices of the means of production impacting firms throughout the economy. This adds to movements in prices at the firm level due to innovation, and to movements in prices at the industry level due to creative destruction. The structure of production and the pattern of consumer expenditure change, leading to obsolescence of capital equipment and labour skills. Aggregate price indices imperfectly capture changes in the price level due to changing relative prices, invalidating meaningful comparisons over long periods for aggregate output, the real wage, and the material standard of living. Evolutionary price theory is a theory of the heterogeneous movement in prices, not a theory of stationary general equilibrium or steady-state growth.

8.2 Areas for Further Research

Analyses in previous chapters identify a variety of mechanisms applying to price determination in an evolving economy. Identifying gaps that remain in the analysis is aided by classifying the mechanisms according to two distinguishing characteristics. Table 1 depicts the classification. One distinguishing characteristic is whether firms are price takers or price makers, while the second is whether the market in which they operate is orderly or disrupted by differential firm growth.

Table 1 Mechanisms for price determination

	Orderly markets	**Disrupted markets**
Price-taker firms	Market-clearing price (Section 4.2)	Balancing capacity expansion with demand growth (Section 5.2.1)
Price-maker firms	Cost-based pricing rules (Section 4.3)	Prices set to finance capacity growth equal to expected demand growth (Section 5.2.2)

Each of the mechanisms of price determination in Table 1 is analysed separately. However, they are all part of a process of economic development that includes transitions between mechanisms. Analysis of the transitions is a proper part of a comprehensive evolutionary price theory.

Creative destruction as analysed in Section 5.2.3 is an example of a transition process between categories of pricing mechanisms. With differential firm growth the market shares of relatively high-cost firms decline while low-cost firms become dominant. As the share-weighted variance in unit cost falls, the driving force of disruption of the market eases.

Innovation results in disruption of orderly markets. Section 3.2.4 discusses factors affecting firm orientation towards innovation. Section 5.1 argues innovation throughout the economy is encouraged by reliable price information coming from orderly markets. All this is sketchy. Research drawing on case studies of innovation is worthwhile for deepening the theory of the role of prices in the transition from orderly to disrupted markets.

Chapter 3 discusses the behaviour of price-taker and price-maker firms without explaining how some firms come to be price takers, while others are price makers. Implicitly, the firm's organisational structure, history, and institutional setting are influences. The relationship between firms also matters, as is clear in the case of price leadership. Explicitly theorising the process determining whether a firm is a price taker or a price maker is a topic worthy of further research.

Table 1 shows price determination in markets with price-taker firms is analysed by balancing supply and demand. A related assumption of pricing to balance the growth of supply with the expected growth of demand is applied to disrupted markets with price-maker firms. These are simplifying, but restrictive, assumptions for thinking through the implications of firm behaviour for market outcomes. Dropping assumed balance in favour of allowing for excess demand or unutilised capacity, as occurs with the analysis price-maker firms in orderly markets, is a worthwhile step towards generalising the evolutionary theory of price determination.

A weakness in the analysis of price determination in markets with differential firm growth in Chapter 5 is the assumption that the pricing routines of firms are unchanged over time. Firm pricing routines coevolve with market structure. In Section 5.3, integrating analysis of changes in firm pricing routines and the evolution of industry structure is suggested as a useful direction for future research in evolutionary price theory. The work of business historians and management scholars provides a fertile ground for appreciative theorising on this topic.

Hints about integrating analysis of changes in pricing routines with the evolution of industry structure are provided in Section 3.4, where pricing routines change over the origination, adoption, and retention phases for introduction of a novel product. Also relevant is Steindl's (1976) post-Keynesian analysis of differential firm growth, which has firm pricing routines becoming less aggressive with increasing industry concentration. Recent works featuring coevolution of pricing routines, consumer behaviour, and market structure include Markey-Towler (2016) and Almudi et al. (2020). More research on this topic is worthwhile.

Investment routines are unchanged over time in analysing differential firm growth in Chapter 5, which ignores the potential co-evolution of investment routines and industry structure. In addition to pricing routines becoming less aggressive with rising industry concentration, Steindl (1976) has firms reducing the amount of profit invested in capacity expansion. A useful direction for further research is deepening the links among investment routines, pricing routines, and the evolution of industry structure. Bloch and Kriesler (2023) review post-Keynesian analysis on linking pricing to the investment decision.

Metcalfe (2025) suggests a need for extending analysis of pricing with differential firm growth beyond an unchanging group of firms, whose expansion is proportional to their profits. New entrants are a source of imitators to accelerate the diffusion of innovations through external financing of investment in productive capacity. Firms diversifying from related industries are a further source of expansion through imitation. Financing of innovation and its diffusion using external sources, including firms diversifying from other industries, is discussed in Minsky (1990), Knell (2015) and Callegari (2018). Further developing the role of entry and external finance in the analysis of differential firm growth is a prime topic for further research.

Nelson (2020) observes studies of productivity growth at the firm and industry levels show improvements in productivity within firms account for a larger proportion of increases in industry average productivity than does the selection of firms through differential firm growth. Learning and competitive pressure are important drivers of productivity improvement at the firm level (see Downie (1958) for an early discussion). There is also a bias in the measurement of productivity growth at the firm level. Relative prices of high-cost firms rise with differential firm growth in the analysis of Section 5.2.2. A rising relative price is measured as a rise in real output when the value of output of a high-cost firm is deflated by the share-weighted price for the industry. A topic worthy of further research is the implications of evolutionary price theory for the measurement of productivity growth at the micro, meso, and macro levels.

The scope of this Element is limited. Discussion of applications to empirical research is restricted to a few peripheral comments. How evolutionary price theory might guide economic policy is not discussed. Developing the implications of evolutionary price theory for empirical research and economic policy are prospective topics for further research.

8.3 Final Observations

Evolutionary price theory provides a framework for analysing the dual role of prices in capitalist economies. Prices coordinate mutually beneficial exchanges between buyers and sellers. They also provide information to entrepreneurs to evaluate the profitability of potential innovations arising from human creativity and restless knowledge. Market capitalism is self-ordering and self-transforming, with prices playing an essential role.

Evolutionary price theory abandons the pursuit of a universal science of human economic behaviour that characterises mainstream economics, instead incorporating history and institutions into the analysis of economic activity. An open-systems ontology is employed in place of the closed-system ontology of the mainstream. Furthermore, a micro-meso-macro methodology is used in place of the methodological individualism used in mainstream economics.

Evolutionary price theory has consumers and firms operating according to habits, rules, and routines, rather than assuming optimising behaviour based on the Olympian rationality of mainstream economics. These habits, rules, and routines are reasoned, but imperfect, responses to limited cognition, incomplete knowledge and connections, and an uncertain, indeed unknowable, future. They change with learning and imagination, so they are historically and institutionally specific, co-evolving with institutions and society.

Learning improves the operations of consumers and firms, while entrepreneurial action adds novelty to the market environment. Markets provide a testing ground to sort the wheat from the chaff. Winners expand relative to the losers, increasing the average fitness of the population. However, sorting using the market mechanism with creative destruction comes at a cost to society in terms of obsolete capital equipment and skills. Just as capital is created when bankers extend newly created credit to entrepreneurs and the market validates this capital by profits to the entrepreneur, capital is destroyed when the entrepreneurs drop prices to aggressively to expand their market share. Mainstream economics is silent on such dynamics because all firms are assumed to be identical and operated optimally, which rules out creative destruction.

Evolutionary price theory treats competition as a process unlike the structure-conduct-performance approach of mainstream economics. In the differential firm growth analysis of Chapter 5, prices fall with rising industry concentration as market share shifts from high-cost firms to low-cost firms. Innovation leads to new products and, eventually, to new industries along the meso-trajectory of origination, adoption, and retention, with prices declining as firms adopt more aggressive pricing routines to expand their market.

Schumpeter's ([1950] 1976, p. 85) view of the competitive process remains relevant, 'it becomes a matter of comparative indifference whether competition in the ordinary sense functions more or less promptly; the powerful lever that in the long run expands output and brings down prices is in any case made of other stuff.' The competition that counts comes from new products, new production processes, and new ways of organising distribution, witness mobile versus landline telephony, electricity from solar panels and wind turbines versus coal-fired generating plants, and ecommerce versus bricks-and-mortar retailing.

Evolutionary price theory analyses the determination of prices in an economy that is growing through innovation and structural change. It is a theory of the movement of prices through time rather than a theory of the structure of prices in the short or long run as in mainstream economics. The process occurs unevenly over time, is irreversible and path dependent. The pattern and content of the economic order is continually transformed, creating worlds we then lose.[37]

The heterogeneity of firms and consequent price dynamics are at centre stage. Some industries are directly impacted, while other industries face changes in the prices of inputs and the prices of competing products. The process is locally degenerative, with shrinking market shares of unfit firms consuming the heterogeneity that drives differential firm growth. However, entrepreneurial actions based on restless knowledge, creativity, and imagination ensure that variety is replenished. Development from within continues indefinitely. Evolutionary price theory provides the framework for analysing how prices guide and are impacted by this process.

---

[37] Alchian (1950) treats the market as the arena in which unfit innovations are eliminated, but fails to recognise the role of the price system in generating innovations in a full evolutionary dynamic.

References

Acs, Zoltan J. and David B. Audretsch (1988), 'Innovation in large and small firms: An empirical analysis', *American Economic Review*, 78(4): 678–690.

Alchian, Armen (1950), 'Uncertainty, evolution and economic theory', *Journal of Political Economy*, 58(3): 211–221.

Almudi, Isabel and Francisco Fatas-Villafranca (2021), *Coevolution in Economic Systems*, Cambridge, Cambridge University Press.

Almudi, Isabel, Francisco Fatas-Villafranca, Jesus Palacio and Julio Sanchez-Choliz (2020), 'Pricing routines and industrial dynamics', *Journal of Evolutionary Economics*, 30(3): 705–739.

Andersen, Esben S. (2012), 'Schumpeter's core works revisited – resolved problems and remaining challenges', *Journal of Evolutionary Economics*, 22(4): 627–648.

Arrow, Kenneth (1974), *The Limits of Organization*, New York, Norton.

Arthur, W. Brian (2015), *Complexity and the Economy*, Oxford, Oxford University Press.

Asimakopoulos, Anthony (1975), 'A Kaleckian theory of income distribution', *Canadian Journal of Economics*, 8(3): 313–333.

Aspromourgos, Tony, Kenji Mori, Masashi Morioka. et al. (2022), 'Symposium on Yoshinori Shiozawa, Masashi Morioka and Kazuhisa Taniguchi (2019), *Microfoundations of Evolutionary Economics*, Springer, Tokyo: Japan', *Metroeconomica*, 73: 2–48.

Bain, Joe S. (1956), *Barriers to New Competition*, Cambridge, MA, Harvard University Press.

Barnard, Chester I. ([1938] 1966), *The Functions of the Executive*, Cambridge, MA, Harvard University Press.

Barney, Jay, (1991), 'Firm resources and sustained competitive advantage', *Journal of Management*, 17, 99–120.

Baumol, William J. (1958), 'On the theory of oligopoly', *Economica*, 25, 187–198.

Baumol, William J., John C. Panzar and Robert D. Willig (1982), *Contestable Markets and the Theory of Industry Structure*, New York, Harcourt Brace Jovanovich.

Berle, Adolf A. and Gardiner C. Means (1932), *The Modern Corporation and Private Property*, New York, Macmillan.

Bloch, Harry (1981), 'Determinants of the variance of market shares in Canadian manufacturing', *Journal of Industrial Economics*, 29(4): 385–393.

Bloch, Harry (1990), 'Price leadership and the degree of monopoly', *Journal of Post Keynesian Economics*, 12(3): 439–451.

Bloch, Harry (2000), 'Schumpeter and Steindl on the dynamics of competition', *Journal of Evolutionary Economics*, 10(3): 343–353.

Bloch, Harry (2005), 'Steindl's analysis of firm growth and the tendency toward industry concentration', in Tracy Mott and Nina Shapiro, editors, *Rethinking Capitalist Development: Essays on the Economics of Joseph Steindl*, London, Routledge: 23–36.

Bloch, Harry (2016a), 'Prices in motion: Schumpeter's contribution to price theory', *Metroeconomica*, 67(4): 742–767.

Bloch, Harry (2016b), 'Post Keynesian price theory with a Schumpeterian twist', in Jerry Courvisanos, James Doughney and Alex Millmow, editors, *Reclaiming Pluralism for Economics*, London, Routledge: 203–220.

Bloch, Harry (2018a), *Schumpeter's Price Theory*, London, Routledge.

Bloch, Harry (2018b), 'Neo-Schumpeterian price theory with Sraffian and post-Keynesian elements', *Journal of Evolutionary Economics*, 28(5): 1035–1051.

Bloch, Harry (2018c), 'Innovation and industry evolution', *International Journal of the Economics of Business*, 25(1): 73–83.

Bloch, Harry (2020), 'Price theory historically considered: Smith, Ricardo, Marshall and beyond', *History of Economics Review*, 75: 50–73.

Bloch, Harry (2022), 'The language of pluralism from the history of the theory of price determination: Natural price, equilibrium price and administered price', *Metroeconomica*, 73(4): 1094–1111.

Bloch, Harry and John Finch (2010), 'Firms and industries in evolutionary economics: Lessons from Marshall, Young, Steindl and Penrose', *Journal of Evolutionary Economics*, 20(1): 139–162.

Bloch, Harry and Peter Kriesler (2023), 'Revisiting "Pricing and the investment decision"', *Review of Political Economy*, published online 12 December 2023, http://doi.org/10.1080/09538259.2023.2283750.

Bloch, Harry and Stan Metcalfe (2011), 'Complexity in the theory of the developing firm', in Cristiano Antonelli, editor, *Handbook on the Economic Complexity of Technological Change*, Cheltenham, Edward Elgar: 81–104.

Bloch, Harry and Stan Metcalfe (2015), 'Restless knowledge, capabilities and the nature of the mega-firm', in Andreas Pyka and John Foster, editors, *The Evolution of Economic and Innovation Systems*, Heidelberg, Springer: 431–453.

Bloch, Harry and Stan Metcalfe (2018), 'Innovation, creative destruction and price theory', *Industrial and Corporate Change*, 27(1): 1–13.

Bloch, Harry and Stan Metcalfe (2024), 'Price theory in a complex and evolving economy', in Ping Chen, Wolfram Elsner, Andreas Pyka, editors, *Handbook of Complexity Economics*, London, Routledge: 292–304.

Bloch, Harry and David Sapsford (2004), 'Commodity prices, wages and U.S. inflation in the twentieth century', *Journal of Post Keynesian Economics*, 26(3): 523–545.

Bloch, Harry and David Sapsford (2013), 'Innovation, real primary commodity prices and business cycles', in Esben Andersen and Andreas Pyka, editors, *Long Term Economic Development – Demand, Finance, Organization, Policy and Innovation in a Schumpeterian Perspective*, Berlin, Springer: 175–189.

Callegari, Beniamio (2018), 'The finance/innovation nexus in Schumpeterian analysis: Theory and application in the case of U.S. trustified capitalism', *Journal of Evolutionary Economics*, 28(5): 1175–1198.

Chai, Andreas and Zakaria Babutsidze (2024), 'Evolutionary consumer theory', in Kurt Dopfer, Richard R. Nelson, Jason Potts and Andreas Pyka, editors, *Routledge Handbook of Evolutionary Economics*, London, Routledge: 261–283.

Chandler, Alfred (1962), *Strategy and Structure: Chapters in the History of Industrial Enterprise*, Cambridge, MA, MIT Press.

Chandler, Alfred (1977), *The Visible Hand: The Managerial Revolution in American Business*, Cambridge, MA, Harvard University Press.

Chatterjee, Rabikar (2009). 'Strategic pricing of new products and services', in Vithala R. Rao, editor, *Handbook of Pricing Research in Marketing*, Cheltenham, Edward Elgar: 169–215.

Coad, Alex (2009), *The Growth of Firms: A Survey of Theories and Empirical Evidence*, Cheltenham, Edward Elgar.

Coase, Ronald H. (1937), 'The nature of the firm', *Economica*, 4: 386–405.

Coase, Ronald H. (1988), 'The nature of the firm: influence', *Journal of Law, Economics and Organization*, 4: 33–47

Cyert, Richard M. and James G. March (1963), *Behavioral Theory of the Firm*, Englewood Cliffs, NJ, Prentice-Hall.

Dean, Joel (1969), 'Pricing pioneering products', *Journal of Industrial Economics*, 17(3): 165–179.

Dopfer, Kurt (2001), 'History-friendly theories in economics: Reconciling universality and context in evolutionary analysis', in John Foster and J. Stanley Metcalfe, editors, *Frontiers of Evolutionary Economics: Competition, Self-Organization and Innovation Policy*, Cheltenham, Edward Elgar: 160–187.

Dopfer, Kurt, John Foster and Jason Potts (2004), 'Micro-meso-macro', *Journal of Evolutionary* Economics, 14(3): 263–279.

Dopfer, Kurt and Jason Potts (2008), *The General Theory of Economic Evolution*, London, Routledge.

Dosi, Giovanni, Richard R. Nelson and Sidney G. Winter (2002), *The Nature and Dynamics of Organizational Capabilities*, Oxford, Oxford University Press.

Downie, Jack (1958), *The Competitive Process*, London, Duckworth.

Downward, Paul (1999), *Pricing Theory in Post Keynesian Economics*, Cheltenham, Edward Elgar.

Duesenberry, James S. (1949), *Income, Saving and the Theory of Consumption Behavior*. Cambridge, MA, Harvard University Press.

Earl, Peter (2022), *Principles of Behavioural Economics: Bringing Together Old, New and Evolutionary Approaches*, Cambridge, Cambridge University Press.

Earl, Peter (2023), 'Rules all the way down: Consumer behaviour from the standpoint of the "ONE behavioural" research programme', *Journal of Consumer Behavior*, 22: 1–16.

Eaton, B. Curtis and Richard G. Lipsey (1980), 'Exit barriers are entry barriers: The durability of capital as a barrier to entry', *Bell Journal of Economics*, 11(2): 721–729.

Eichner, Alfred S. (1973), 'A theory of the determination of the mark-up under oligopoly', *Economic Journal*, 83: 1184–1200.

Eichner, Alfred S. (1976), *The Megacorp and Oligopoly*, Armonk, M.E. Sharpe.

Eichner, Alfed S. (1985), *Towards a New Economics: Essays in Post-Keynesian and Institutionalist Theory*, Armonk, M.E. Sharpe.

Eliasson, Gunnar (2024), 'The firm as an experimental decision maker', in Kurt Dopfer, Richard R. Nelson, Jason Potts and Andreas Pyka, editors, *Routledge Handbook of Evolutionary Economics*, London, Routledge: 185–196.

Ezekiel, Mordecai (1938), 'The cobweb theorem', *Quarterly Journal of Economics*, 52(2): 255–280.

Foster, John (2000), 'Competitive selection, self-organisation and Joseph A. Schumpeter', *Journal of Evolutionary Economics*, 10(3): 311–328.

Foster, John (2005), 'From simplistic to complex systems in economics', *Cambridge Journal of Economics*, 29: 873–892.

Foster, John (2021), The US consumption function: A new perspective', *Journal of Evolutionary Economics*, 31(3): 773–798.

Freeman, Christopher and Francisco Louçã (2001), *As Time Goes By – From the Industrial Revolutions to the Information Revolution*, Oxford, Oxford University Press.

Gallegati, Marco (2019), 'A system for dating long wave phases in economic development', *Journal of Evolutionary Economics*, 29(3): 803–822.

Garegnani, Pierangelo (1990), 'Sraffa: classical versus marginalist analysis', in Krishna Bharadwaj and Bertram Schefold, editors, *Essays on Piero Sraffa*, London, Routledge: 112–141.

Gustafsson, Robin, Mikko Jääskeläinen, Markku Mauls and Juha Uotila (2016), 'Emergence of industries: A review and future directions', *International Journal of Management Reviews*, 18(1): 28–50.

Hall, Robert L. and Charles J. Hitch (1939), 'Price theory and business behaviour', *Oxford Economic Papers*, 2: 12–45.

Harcourt, Geoffrey C. and Peter Kenyon (1976), 'Pricing and the investment decision', *Kyklos*, 29(3): 449–477.

Hayek, Friedrich A. (1935), *Prices and Production*, London, Routledge and Kegan Paul.

Hayek, Friedrich A. (1948), *Individualism and Economic Order*, London, Routledge and Kegan Paul.

Hodgson, Geoffrey M. (1997), 'The ubiquity of habits and rules', *Cambridge Journal of Economics*, 21: 663–684.

Hunt, E. Kdward (1979), *History of Economic Thought: A Critical Perspective*, Belmont, CA, Wadsworth.

Innis, Harold A. (1940), 'Review of *Business Cycles: A Theoretical, Historical and Statistical Analysis of Capitalist Process* by Joseph A. Schumpeter', *Canadian Journal of Economics and Political Science*, 6(1): 90–96.

Kaldor, Nicholas (1934), 'A classificatory note of the determinateness of equilibrium', *Review of Economic Studies*, 1(2): 122–136.

Kaldor, Nicholas (1985), *Economics without Equilibrium*, Cardiff, University College Cardiff Press.

Kalecki, Michał (1937), 'The principle of increasing risk', *Economica*, 3, 440–447.

Kalecki, Michał (1971), *Selected Essays on the Dynamics of the Capitalist Economy*, Cambridge, Cambridge University Press.

Kay, John (2018), 'Theories of the firm', *International Journal of the Economics of Business*, 25(1): 11–17.

Keynes, John M. (1930), 'Economics possibilities for our grandchildren', *The Nation and Anthenaeum*, 48(2): 36–37, 48(3): 96–98. Reprinted in Keynes, John M. (1932), *Essays in Economic Persuasion*, New York, Harcourt Brace: 358–373.

Kirman, Alan (2011), *Complex Economics: Individual and Collective Rationality*, London, Routledge.

Knell, Mark (2015), 'Schumpeter, Keynes and the financial instability hypothesis', *Journal of Evolutionary Economics*, 25(1): 293–310.

Knight, Frank H. ([1921] 1971), *Risk, Uncertainty and Profit*, Chicago, University of Chicago Press.

Kondratieff, Nikolai D. (1935), 'The long waves of economic life', *Review of Economics and Statistics*, 17(6): 105–115.

Kriesler, Peter (1987), *Kalecki's Microanalysis*, Cambridge, Cambridge University Press.

Kurz, Heinz D. (2008), 'Innovations and profits: Schumpeter and the classical heritage', *Journal of Economic and Behavioral Organization*, 67(1): 263–278.

Kuznets, Simon (1940), 'Schumpeter's *Business Cycles*', *American Economic Review*, 30: 257–271.

Lavoie, Marc (2022), *Post-Keynesian Economics: New Foundations*, Cheltenham, Edward Elgar.

Lee, Frederic S. (1999), *Post Keynesian Pricing Theory*, Cambridge, Cambridge University Press.

Leontief, Wasily (1986), 'Input-output analysis', in Wasily Leontief, editor, *Input-Output Economics*, Oxford, Oxford University Press.

Levine, David P. (1997), 'Knowing and acting: On uncertainty in economics', *Review of Political Economy*, 9: 5–17.

Lipsey, Richard G., Carlaw, Kenneth I. and Bekar, Clifford T. (2005), *Economic Transformations*, Oxford, Oxford University Press.

Loasby, Brian J. (1999), *Knowledge, Institutions and Evolution in Economics*, London, Routledge.

Loasby, Brian J. (2003), 'Efficiency and time', in Richard Arena and Michel Quere, editors, *The Economics of Alfred Marshall: Revisiting Marshall's Legacy*, London, Palgrave Macmillan: 202–220.

Louçã, Francisco (2021), 'As time went by – why is the long wave so long?', *Journal of Evolutionary Economics*, 31(3): 749–771.

Malerba, Franco, Richard R. Nelson, Luigi Orsenigo and Sydney G. Winter (1999), 'History-friendly models of industry evolution: The computer industry', *Industry and Corporate Change*, 8(1): 3–4.

Malthus, Thomas ([1798] 1991), *An Essay on the Principle of Population*, Oxford, Oxford University Press.

Markey-Towler, Brendan (2016), 'Law of the jungle: Firm survival and price dynamics in evolutionary markets', *Journal of Evolutionary Economics*, 26(3): 655–696.

Marris, Robin (1964), *The Theory of Managerial Capitalism*, London, Macmillan.
Marshall, Alfred (1920), *Principles of Economics*, 8th ed., London, Macmillan.
Marshall, Alfred (1923), *Industry and Trade*, 4th ed., London, Macmillan.
Marx, Karl ([1887] 1954), *Capital, Volume 1*, Moscow, Progress Publishers.
Melmiès, Jordan (2023), 'Unit profit margins along post-Keynesian lines: From Sraffa, Kalecki, Robinson to Eichner, Wood, Harcourt and Kenyon', *European Journal of the History of Economic Thought*, 30(1): 1–21. https://doi.org/10.1080/09672567.2022.2098998.
Metcalfe, J. Stanley (1998), *Evolutionary Economics and Creative Destruction*, London, Routledge.
Metcalfe, J. Stanley (2001), 'Consumption, preferences and the evolutionary agenda', *Journal of Evolutionary Economics*, 11(1): 37–58.
Metcalfe, J. Stanley (2007), 'Alfred Marshall's Mecca: Reconciling the theories of value and development', *Economic Record*, 83(supplement): S1–S22.
Metcalfe, J. Stanley (2008), 'The broken thread: Marshall, Schumpeter and Hayek on the evolution of capitalism', in Yuichi Shinoya and Tomatsu Nishizawa, editors, *Marshall and Schumpeter on Evolution*, Cheltenham, Edward Elgar: 116–144.
Metcalfe, Stan (2025), 'The innovation-competition connection', in Kurt Dopfer, editor, *Elgar Research Agenda for Evolutionary Economics*, Cheltenham, Edward Elgar, forthcoming.
Minsky, Hyman P. (1990), 'Schumpeter: Finance and evolution', in Arnold Heertje and Mark Perlman, editors, *Evolving Technology and Market Structure*, Ann Arbor, University of Michigan Press: 51–74.
Nelson, Richard R. (1991), 'Why do firms differ; and how does it matter', *Strategic Journal of Management*, 12, 61–74.
Nelson, Richard R. (2008), 'Why do firms differ and how does it matter? A revisitation', *Seoul Journal of Economics*, 21(4): 607–619.
Nelson, Richard R. (2013), 'Demand, supply, and their interaction on markets, as seen from the perspective of evolutionary economic theory', *Journal of Evolutionary Economics*, 23(1): 17–38.
Nelson, Richard R. (2020), 'A perspective on the evolution of evolutionary economics', *Industrial and Corporate Change*, 29(5): 1101–1118.
Nelson, Richard R. and Davide Consoli (2010), 'An evolutionary theory of household consumption behavior', *Journal of Evolutionary Economics*, 20(3): 665–687.
Nelson, Richard R. and Sidney G. Winter (1982), *An Evolutionary Theory of Economic Change*, Cambridge, MA, Harvard University Press.

Oakley, Allen (1990), *Schumpeter's Theory of Capitalist Motion: A Critical Exposition and Reassessment*, Aldershot, Hants, Edward Elgar.

Pasinetti, Luigi (1977), *Lectures in the Theory of Production*, New York, Columbia University Press.

Pasinetti, Luigi L. (1981), *Structural Change and Economic Growth*, Cambridge, Cambridge University Press.

Penrose, Edith (1959), *The Theory of the Growth of the Firm*, Oxford, Basil Blackwell.

Perez, Carlota (2002), *Technological Revolutions and Financial Capital*, Cheltenham, Edward Elgar.

Phelps, Edmund and Sidney Winter (1970), 'Optimal price policy under atomistic competition', in Edmund Phelps, editor, *Micro Economic Foundations of Employment and Inflation Theory*, New York, W. Norton: 309–337.

Pigou, Alfred C. (1920), *The Economics of Welfare*, London, Macmillan.

Porter, Michael (1985), *Competitive Advantage, Creating and Sustaining Superior Performance*, New York, Free Press.

Potts, Jason (2000), *The New Evolutionary Microeconomics*, Cheltenham, Edward Elgar.

Potts, Jason (2001), 'Knowledge and markets', *Journal of Evolutionary Economics*, 11(4): 413–431.

Potts, Jason (2017), 'Institutions hold consumption on a leash: An evolutionary approach to the future of consumption', *Journal of Evolutionary Economics*, 27(2): 239–250.

Ricardo, David ([1821] 1973), *The Principles of Political Economy*, London, Dent.

Robinson, Edward A. G. (1931), *The Structure of Competitive Industry*, Cambridge, Cambridge University Press.

Roncaglia, Alessandro (1978), *Sraffa and the Theory of Prices*, Chichester, UK, John Wiley and Sons.

Roncaglia, Alessandro (2006), *The Wealth of Ideas: A History of Economic Thought*, Cambridge, Cambridge University Press.

Rosenberg, Hans (1940), 'Review of *Business Cycles: A Theoretical, Historical and Statistical Analysis of Capitalist Process* by Joseph A. Schumpeter', *American Historical Review*, 46(1): 96–99.

Salter, Wilfred E. G. (1966), *Productivity and Technical Change*, Cambridge, Cambridge University Press.

Schumpeter, Joseph A. ([1934] 1961), *The Theory of Economic Development: An Inquiry into Profits, Credit, Interest, and the Business Cycle*, translation of second German edition of Schumpeter (1926) by Redvers Opie, London, Oxford University Press.

Schumpeter, Joseph A. (1939), *Business Cycles: A Theoretical, Historical and Statistical Analysis of the Capitalist Process*, Volumes 1 and 2, New York, McGraw-Hill.

Schumpeter, Joseph A. (1947), 'The creative response in economic history', *Journal of Economic History*, 7(2): 149–159.

Schumpeter, Joseph A. (1949), 'The historical approach to the analysis of business cycles', *Universities-National Bureau Conference on Business Cycle Research*, November 25–27. Reprinted in Schumpeter (1951): 308–315.

Schumpeter, Joseph A. ([1950] 1976), *Capitalism, Socialism and Democracy*, 3rd ed., New York, Harper and Row.

Schumpeter, Joseph A. (1951), *Essays of J.A. Schumpeter*, edited by Richard V. Clemence, Cambridge, MA, Addison-Wesley Press.

Schumpeter, Joseph A. (1954), *History of Economic Analysis*, Oxford, Oxford University Press.

Schumpeter, Joseph A. (1970), *Das Wesen des Geldes*, edited by Fritz Mann from a 1930 unpublished manuscript, Gottingen, Vandenhoeck and Ruprecht.

Schumpeter, Joseph A. (2014), *Treatise on Money*, English translation by Reuben Alvarado of Schumpeter (1970), Aalten, Woodbridge.

Shackle, George L. S. (1959), 'The complex nature of time as a concept in economics', *Economia Internazionale*, 7(4): 743–757.

Shackle, George L. S. (1970), *Expectation, Enterprise and Profit*, London: George Allen and Unwin.

Shiller, Robert J. (2000), *Irrational Exuberance*, Princeton, NJ: Princeton University Press.

Shiozawa, Yoshinori, Masashi Morioka and Kazuhisa Taniguchi (2019). *Microfoundations of Evolutionary Economics*, Tokyo, Springer Japan.

Simon, Herbert (1955), 'A behavioural model of rational choice', *Quarterly Journal of Economics*, 69: 99–118.

Simon, Herbert (1964), 'On the concept of an organizational goal', *Administrative Science Quarterly*, 9: 1–22.

Smith, Adam ([1776] 1937), *An Inquiry into the Nature and Causes of the Wealth of Nations*, New York, Random House.

Sraffa, Piero (1960), *Production of Commodities by Means of Commodities*, Cambridge, Cambridge University Press.

Steindl, Josef (1945), *Small and Big Business: Economic Problems of the Size of Firms*, Oxford, Blackwell.

Steindl, Josef (1976), *Maturity and Stagnation in American Capitalism*, 2nd ed., New York, Monthly Review Press.

Sutton, John (1991), *Sunk Costs and Market Structure: Price Competition, Advertising, and the Evolution of Concentration*, Cambridge, MA, MIT Press.

Sutton, John (1998), *Technology and Market Structure: Theory and History*, Cambridge, MA, MIT Press.

Sylos-Labini, Paolo (1962), *Oligopoly and Technical Progress*, Cambridge, MA, Harvard University Press.

Sylos-Labini, Paolo (1984), *The Forces of Economic Growth and Decline*, Cambridge, MA, MIT Press.

Syverson, Chad (2011), 'What determines productivity?' *Journal of Economic Literature*, 49(2): 326–365.

Taylor, Frederick W. (1911), *The Principles of Scientific Management*, New York, Harper and Brothers.

Teece, David (2009), *Dynamic Capabilities and Strategic Management*, Oxford, Oxford University Press.

Teece, David (2024), 'Evolutionary economics, routines and dynamic capabilities', in Kurt Dopfer, Richard R. Nelson, Jason Potts and Andreas Pyka, editors, *Routledge Handbook of Evolutionary Economics*, London, Routledge: 197–214.

Tylecote, Andrew (1992), *The Long Wave in the World Economy*, London, Routledge.

Veblen, Thorsten (1899), *The Theory of the Leisure Class: an Economic Study of Institutions*, London, Macmillan.

Wang, Yangyuzi (2024), 'Stability of price and quantity to a long-run equilibrium: A dynamic Leontief model with bounded rationality', *Evolutionary and Institutional Economics Review*, published online 26 April 2024, https://doi.org/10.1007/s40844-024-00282-2.

Winter, Sidney (2006), 'Toward a neo-Schumpeterian theory of the firm', *Industrial and Corporate Change*, 15: 125–141.

Witt, Ulrich (2001), 'Learning to consume – a theory of wants and the growth of demand', *Journal of Evolutionary Economics*, 11(1): 23–36.

Wood, Adrian (1975), *A Theory of Profits*, Cambridge, Cambridge University Press.

Ziman, John (1978), *Reliable Knowledge: An Exploration of the Grounds for Scientific Belief*, Cambridge, Cambridge University Press.

Cambridge Elements

Evolutionary Economics

John Foster
University of Queensland

John Foster is Emeritus Professor of Economics and former Head of the School of Economics at the University of Queensland, Brisbane. He is Fellow of the Academy of Social Science in Australia, Life member of Clare Hall College, Cambridge and Past President of the International J.A. Schumpeter Society.

Jason Potts
RMIT University

Jason Potts is Professor of Economics at RMIT University, Melbourne. He is also an Adjunct Fellow at the Institute of Public Affairs. His research interests include technological change, economics of innovation, and economics of cities. He was the winner of the 2000 International Joseph A. Schumpeter Prize and has published over 60 articles and six books.

Isabel Almudi
University of Zaragoza

Isabel Almudi is Professor of Economics at the University of Zaragoza, Spain, where she also belongs to the Instituto de Biocomputación y Física de Sistemas Complejos. She has been Visiting Fellow at the European University Institute, Columbia University and RMIT University. Her research fields are evolutionary economics, innovation studies, environmental economics and dynamic systems.

Francisco Fatas-Villafranca
University of Zaragoza

Francisco Fatas-Villafranca is Professor of Economics at the University of Zaragoza, Spain. He has been Visiting Scholar at Columbia University and Visiting Researcher at the University of Manchester. His research focuses on economic theory and quantitative methods in the social sciences, with special interest in evolutionary economics.

David A. Harper
New York University

David A. Harper is Clinical Professor of Economics and Co-Director of the Program on the Foundations of the Market Economy at New York University. His research interests span institutional economics, Austrian economics and evolutionary economics. He has written two books and has published extensively in academic journals. He was formerly Chief Analyst and Manager at the New Zealand Treasury.

About the Series

Cambridge Elements of Evolutionary Economics provides authoritative and up-to-date reviews of core topics and recent developments in the field. It includes state-of-the-art contributions on all areas in the field. The series is broadly concerned with questions of dynamics and change, with a particular focus on processes of entrepreneurship and innovation, industrial and institutional dynamics, and on patterns of economic growth and development.

Cambridge Elements

Evolutionary Economics

Elements in the Series

A Reconsideration of the Theory of Non-Linear Scale Effects: The Sources of Varying Returns to, and Economies of, Scale
Richard G. Lipsey

Evolutionary Economics: Its Nature and Future
Geoffrey M. Hodgson

Coevolution in Economic Systems
Isabel Almudi and Francisco Fatas-Villafranca

Industrial Policy: The Coevolution of Public and Private Sources of Finance for Important Emerging and Evolving Technologies
Kenneth I. Carlaw and Richard G. Lipsey

Explaining Technology
Roger Koppl, Roberto Cazzolla Gatti, Abigail Devereaux, Brian D. Fath, James Herriot, Wim Hordijk, Stuart Kauffman, Robert E. Ulanowicz and Sergi Valverde

Evolutionary Games and the Replicator Dynamics
Saul Mendoza-Palacios and Onésimo Hernández-Lerma

The Dynamic Metacapabilities Framework: Introducing Quantum Management and the Informational View of the Firm
Harold Paredes-Frigolett and Andreas Pyka

Entrepreneurship and Evolutionary Economics
Per L. Bylund

Agent-based Macroeconomics: The Schumpeter Meeting Keynes Models
Giovanni Dosi and Andrea Roventini

Evolutionary Price Theory
Harry Bloch

A full series listing is available at: www.cambridge.org/EEVE

For EU product safety concerns, contact us at Calle de José Abascal, 56–1º, 28003 Madrid, Spain or eugpsr@cambridge.org.

www.ingramcontent.com/pod-product-compliance
Ingram Content Group UK Ltd.
Pitfield, Milton Keynes, MK11 3LW, UK
UKHW021839150525
458487UK00018B/363